Journey to Love:
A Book of Poems

By
Eunice Moseley, MS, M.B.A.

© 2015 Freelance Associates
Long Beach, CA 90807

To
Bear

TABLE OF CONTENT

I. The Beginning   5

II. Forbidden Friendship   37

III. Under Fire   112

IV. Full Armor   147

Journey To Love: A Book of Poems
By Eunice Moseley, MS, M.B.A.

Chapter I

The Beginning

    This is a true story that sounds so unbelievable it sounds like a lie or my imagination. What is portrayed in public as the truth is really a lie or fabrication of the truth. Sometimes a lie is more realistic than the truth. There is an old saying that "its so crazy it must be the truth." This is my truth.

    It is a journey that started for me in 2011. I got a call from an old friend. At the time I was three years into a Masters degree program at University of Maryland's' online college, and preparing my clients, that I consult in public relations/business management, for my retirement so that I could focus on my classes. I had one other client I was waiting for their retainer to end when I received a phone call that would begin my *Journey to Love*.

    Though a book of poems it is biographically based and I believe it may be the greatest love story every told...if you believe it.

    Through my poems, *Journey to Love...*, I will chronicalizes how two people that weren't looking for love found it in each other. It is also about what they had to go through to keep it.

    My friend's name is Kevin, he started an independent record label with multi-platinum R&B group Dru Hill, and one of the groups' lead singers, SisQo. He wanted to reach another level with Dru Hill, LLC, and needed a discount so I gave them 50% off my normal retainer fee. It included representation as well as consultation. I provided them with a public relations/business strategy. He wanted me to do what he saw me do for my other clients, develop a strategy to make things happen, or as he said, "fill up the holes."

My contact each weekly teleconference was him and SisQo - whom I now call Love. We

> **(July 9, 2011) Friend (Fwd's) SisQo email. It included a link to a video titled "Hide Ya Kids And Hide Ya Husbands! Sisqo (The Dragon) is Back!!!":**
> *"Hey Eunice, is there anything we can do, because these people are crossing the line...thinking about involving attorney, Any thoughts."*
>
> **(July 9, 2011) Me (I am off retainer, which ended in April, 2011:**
> *"Most diff...making false statements that you can not prove is grounds for you to win a slander case. Best way to handle is to sue. To get a reputation as one who will sue you...if you slander their name. SisQo has a good name...except for the baby mamma drama. Paul...in Bmore is my lawyer..ask him for a break."*

discussed implementing the strategy, media issues, and any crisis that came up such as what seemed to me to be an Internet smear campaign against Love by two "gossip" type online media sources.

(Jan. 18, 2011) Me to my Friend:
"...You mentioned plays for SisQo too. I have an interview with David E. Talbert...I will ask him about future placement. He is a long time friend and also graduated from Morgan :)."

(Jan. 18, 2011) Friend:
"That's great David and I went to Morgan together..."

(March 18, 2011) Me:
"Tell SisQo I will present the idea to David about a musical of SisQo play and if he is interested....then give him his draft."

(April 6, 2011) Me:
"...just a reminder....David E. Talbert...stage play does not end until May 8th....doubt he will...discuss it with wife...until after that...so tell SisQo"

(June 23, 2011) Me:
"David...is following me ... on Twitter :)...maybe...he will do SisQo's musica.l (sending up prayers lol)..."

(June 23, 2011) Friend:
"When Prayers go up blessings come down."

We also discussed finding a way into Hollywood so that SisQo could develop several project ideas that he had. I informed them that at a Hollywood Films conference the head executives said they (entertainment personalities like SisQo) had to be current.

So I got the ear to David E. Talbert who I've interviewed for my syndicated column he just signed a movie deal with Fox Searchlight Pictures; Jeff Clanagan at Codeblack, a movie to DVD producer/distributor who just signed a movie production deal with Lionsgate Films, sent a proposals to L'Oreal to pitch SisQo's own signature blond color, mediated a video audition tape to Oprah Winfrey for The Color Purple on Broadway, and sent out a sponsorship proposal to cell phone provider Cricket to sponsor a six-month national tour produced by the group.

We worked together well enough that I was invited to accompany Love and my friend to a social event - the E3 Expo. I coordinated it for them

> **(May 12, 2011) E3 Expo to me (Fwd) to my Friend:**
> *"Hi, I have officially started booking E3 appointments. We'd love for you to spend some time with us at the show."*
>
> **(May 13, 2011) Friend (Fwd) reply from Love:**
> *"Yes, Def this one. Plus fingers crossed for Nintedo, Microsoft & Sony Show."*

even though I was off retainer by then. I discovered slowly in working unofficially with Love how similar he was to my late husband Michael. I started to watch performances via videos placed by fans on Youtube.com because it was hard to believe I had not seen the likeness before.

Love mention to my daughter, who accompanied him to Wilhelmina Talent Agency in Philadelphia, when I had arranged for him to signed on with the agency, that he was dating several women. Said he wanted a reality show about it.

As a PR specialist I saw crisis, but my friend calmed my fears by saying that they knew he was dating others.

By this time I had already let all my clients retainers end without renewal, but told them I would be keeping this new client because he was in dire need of my services, and he was an old friend. I told them also I felt God sent them to me.

I had supplied the PR/business strategy and was trying to get it implemented, but started finding road blocks and experiencing possible sabotage of my moves by the end of the retainer period in April, 2011. I told my friend I been in business long enough to not notice what was happening, or not happening as the case here.

During the first retainer time, which was three months, I sent out those proposals to my contacts acquired via interviewing them throughout my over 20 years as a syndicated columnist (www.ThePulseofEntertainment.com). During that time I was able to get Love signed to one of the largest talent agents in the world, Wilhelmina. A Broadway audition for The Lion King. He sang his solo hit "Incomplete." My friend called me just so I could hear him audition.

Gradually I see that the eventually connected with David E. Talbert, Codeblack,

BET (I also sent the casting director, Robi Reed, a proposal to have the member do cameos), L'Oreal and Cricket. I had put together a 6 month tour for them. - they only needed a $1,000 deposit to lock in tour's first date to snow-ball it. I saw evidence of self produced shows. I was so full with job to see the strategy come together. Disappointed I had not heard from my friend though, I wrote a poem about it "The Honorable Thing."

After the expo I started emailing Love on a personal level while waiting for them to come back on retainer, talking first about his similarities to my mate husband Michael. Then later on because he seemed stressed about something via his Twitter profile. He talked about not being able to breathe, and so he couldn't sing. He talked about his fans being the only ones he could depend on.

> **(July 3, 2011) Me to love:**
> *"Don't have me here worried about you....God put me in your life for a reason. Him nor I ain't going nowhere. He is your air and I am your music. Stay strong. See you soon."*
>
> **(July 5, 2011) Love:**
> *"... thank u for all ur kind words =-)."*

That started the conversations back and forth between us. I started to worry about his mental state. He looked tired I question him?

> **(July 20, 2011) Love from his personal account:**
> *"...I hav a lazy eye ..I'm not tired...lol"*

> **(September 1, 2011) Me replying to Wilhelmina agency (Fwd) to Love (reference to an audition request for "The Good Wife"):**
> *"Hi...not as an extra but thanks for considering him. Thought you had forgot about him :)."*
>
> **(September 1, 2011) Love:**
> *"Kinda sounds like extra work?! Lol"*
>
> **(September 12, 2011) Me to Love about another audition request:**
> *"Somebody is on a roll...looks like its coming from Gillette ...but I am not liking the role."*

His last email reply through his official account was November, 2011, he was asking if I heard about the play. Either he meant Oprah's play or his play that I sent to David E. Talbert to produce - which he said he had to discuss with his wife - who was a fan of Love.

> **(November 2, 2011) Me:**
> *"LA and MD?.... Just read your Twitter. Did you mean Vegas ...?"*
>
> **(November 2, 2011) Love:**
> *"Yes Vegas. Any word on the play?"*

After that day he would only reply directly to my emails via his Twitter. I am still in contact with him by sending him an emails each day, his request through a "ghost" profile. He started shouting me out on stage. He would answer any questions I might ask him or comment on something I said on stage, or in video taped interviews or via his Twitter or Facebook accounts.

Eventually replying to me via his Twitter and Facebook official profiles stopped. He still replies on stage before and between songs, but mainly through his celebrity friends' social media accounts. I am not sure at this point why he stopped speaking to me via his official profiles at that time, but from the back and forth conversations on social media between him and someone else it has to do with a "contract" he signed.

He started to sound very distressed on social media. He would speak to me and someone would post a threat to him, tell him that he couldn't. He was being verbally disrespected too by what seemed like his staff. He was looking really drunk on stage - I became very worried for his emotional state. I started to send a poem a day to lift his spirits.

> **(March 10, 2012) Me to Love:**
> "Saw your message about 'fake' still being around you...that's when I realized that God answered my prayer...I've detached myself from 'that' situation without detaching myself from you...cause I'm not 'seeing' it …"

My friend called came after I had a client (i.e., stage name Trueful) hire Dru Hill for his album release concert at the Los Angeles Convention Center. Since that time I have seen them perform twice more. Once was right after his birthday months after the E3 Expo. It was at the Nokia Theater, and as if it was my show. Seemed like all the members came over to where I was sitting while singing.

Love look and pointed directly at me while singing the lyrics "..and I choose you." The second time was in our hometown of Baltimore at Rams Head Live, while the group was singing "Beauty," he pointed directly at me again while singing the lyrics "...is she over here?"

I started to email him words of encouragement, my philosophies on life, and these poems, I could tell they were working. To see such disrespect of an iconic public figure shocked me. It made me remember what my "third eye" couldn't see at that expo in his stylist, and that my instinct about it had me bothered every since. So I warned him that his troubles with his staff could be evil creating havoc within his circle. I said I would pray for them.

I am a Christian. I am a very Spiritual person with no denomination, but raised in a Baptist church and attended a Catholic Church, while serving in the Navy (I am a disabled veteran). For me life is about serving God or not. Living to serve in God's goodness or living to serve in Satan's evilness.

I had admitted to my friend about why I was apprehensive to come with them to the E3 expo, about his likeness to my late husband. He insisted I come. At the expo I saw that they could have been twins - same body built, height, personality, facial scars, moles, voice, laugh, hands, etc...

I could not take my eyes off him, and I noticed he couldn't take his eyes off me.

I told him later via email how my late husband dreamt that I would meet someone after his death that would look and act just like him. He said him and I would get to raise a son like I always wanted. My late husband said this person and I would live a long and happy life. I believed him for he had proven to me in the 15 years we were together that his dreams would eventually come true.

Through the conversations or communications we found a loving friendship. He asked to "date" me and I said only if I am the only one, because I knew he was dating several. I am also 20 years his senior. I pointed out that he is a public figure, and I am very introvert, shy and have a phobia about having my picture taken - could he deal with that.

He said alright to my "demands" and I think for him he just wanted access to me - I gave him permission. I said I would follow his lead. He said also, "what good is a diamond nobody can see." So I tried to think of ways to get around "my shy issues," such as wearing a big brim fedora (hat) to cover my face. I always use a Chinese hand fan and I thought of using that. I found out later he was able to be with me virtually like when a realtor shows houses via satellite only this is real time via my cell phone number. He explained it to me by sending me a client who explained it to me. When the client never returned I knew why the message was delivered.

Virtually Love saw that my right hand has dark knuckles. I call it my man hand. I tell him it belongs to him and I bet he has a female hand that belong to me. I start to see him and his celebrity friends hiding their knuckles, or with their hands behind them or sticking their hands out there awkwardly. He saw my struggling going up steps (Navy injury); that I wore shades outside - day or night; that I wear a black hootie with sleeves pulled up; that I wear only red lipstick, that I have a crown of grey hair in the front; that without perm my hair is a curly Afro, and with perm its Native Indian straight; that I sleep on a couch; that I use a small heater to keep my injured joints warm, and that I can really dance and love to. His celebrity friends made what he saw the backdrop of their pictures. He saw that I drum on any surface - even my body; that I wear a red watch always; that I drive a little red car (Ford Focus); that I have constant joint pain (Navy Injury); that I wear my purse strap across my chest because of the pain; that because of the injury I fell down the steps landing on my left knee tearing a hole in the knee of my jeans; that I am in college and striving to be a teacher; that I'm scared of the dark and always burn a candle, and that I live on Lime Avenue in a green house by the Beach. All what he sees in my life, virtually, appears in his celebrity friends pictures as back drops or in their poses.

I was reading social media with subtweets bragging about control over them. It seems his former dates could now be either his business partners or have him locked in a contract some how.

Sudden I am being stalked, hacked me, and verbally assaulted. I believe they are using the same technology to stalk me.

They post messages that tell me they are virtually seeing me too. They brag about hacking my computer and stealing my emails with family and clients contact and personal data.

The messages or posts indicate he lost control over his own public image, public associations, public content and public performances schedule. They subtweet to me they plan to publicly make it seem as though he is with someone else, not me. Someone brags its because they are younger and prettier than I.

Soon after Maya Angelo released a video, I thought it strange at the time, she said, "Just because you're pretty doesn't mean you telling the truth, that's just stupid. Shortly after she because sick and passed away.

In social media posted messages via his celebrity friends he assures me there is a deadline to their control.

The last message from my friend Kevin was a text around Christmas, 2011, he said simply, "I made a mistake, please forgive me."

In spite of their situation, what ever it may be, Love and I use the time to get to know each other. He told me to ask him anything, and I asked what did his family call him. I have a family nickname too, Pudden. He told me they call him Bear.

I also asked 'how deep was his love" for me. Him and his group have a song called "How Deep Is Your Love." Soon after I see a new song and music video posted on my Fcebook page timeline of Sean Paul featuring Kelly Rowland (of Destiny's Child) titled "How Deep Is Your Love". The song's lyrics say "mine run down to the Ocean floor." In the video Kelly has hair dye where my grey is and Sean Paul is dressed similar to Love. I wrote a poems about it, "Deep as the Sea."

    The title to this book of poems came from Love. He posted a video once of himself in a recording booth preparing for his current album, and the caption said "Journey to Love." The video was later changed to "Journey to The Last Dragon" - the name of his current project. Since this is dedicated to him I named it *Journey to Love: A Book of Poems,* because all the poems were written to him.

    Recently Michelle Williams (of Destiny's Child) released her new album titled "Journey to Freedom." This happened some time after I started promoting my book's title on my social pages. I believe she follows my Twitter account, knows his situation, and the title is a sort of homage to Love and I. Him and Destiny's Child members go way back to both their music career beginnings.

    Chapter One of *Journey to Love...* is titled "The Beginning," it is my journey from his adviser to his best-friend.

~ ~ ~

Journey To Love: A Book of Poems
By Eunice Moseley, MS, M.B.A.

BOOK OF LIFE

"When your day comes and 'The Author;' writes your story in the Book of Life, what will it say was your legacy, love or hate......for life is but a test to see if without the obvious would you still believe......when life took you to the edge and you didn't know if tomorrow you would eat, did you use hate to put food on the table or did you trust in God and believe......will it say you were fair, helped those in need or will it show a pattern of greed......will the Book of Life say that you loved along the way or will it show evidence of you consistently blocking you brothers way - every single day......when your day comes and The Author reads your Book of Life, will it show that you are an example of how Jesus handled evil through life's turns and twists, will you be a mirror image of Christ showing proof of your personal relationship?..."

AN EVERLASTING LOVE

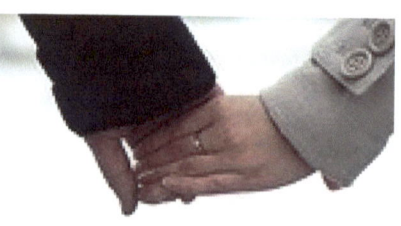

"There's nothing like love when it touches your heart, to know that love means you'll never be apart……a love stronger than any bond made by man, and when all else fails, this love will forever stand……there's nothing like a love that makes you want to trust, make you understand the cards life has dealt, let love play them without a fuss ……that love that takes you as you are, disregards what you're lacking helps you can go far……there's nothing like love when it's returned with just as much passion as you've given, a reinforcement to the power of love insuring you it will be there for as long as you're living…"

~ ~ ~

SEASON OF LOVE

"It's the season for cheer, greeting your neighbors with no fear…..knowing they will respond, everyone showing they care, that's why I love this time of the year……its the spirit of Christ's

love you see, a chance to start a new, as the new year will bring, like Christ an offering of a new beginning......I love this time of the year, the colors so festive in every way, an easy transition to what follows, all red for Valentine's day..."

~ ~ ~

A LITTLE TIME

"Takes a little time but you can get what you want in time, what could be the problem you may later see is that what you wanted wasn't meant to be...... takes a little time but it heals wounds to a dark scare, what could be the problem is people see 'that' as who you are...... takes a little time but the truth shall see the light of day, what could be the problem is some may not like what you have to say......takes a little time but you get to see the human in everyone, what could be the problem is not excepting those faults never knowing you had already won......takes a little time but you get what God promised to you, what could be the problem is not having the patience or faith to step aside and let Him bring it to you.....takes a little time but I'll hold you again, and the only problem will be then, is whether you'll ever let go of me my friend..."

~ ~ ~

JESUS LIKE

"It's Christmas eve the night before we celebrate the birth of a man, one who would turn out to be a symbol of what we - in spite of evil - can be if we take God's hand......We celebrate the life of one, who ended up being God's only beloved son......His birth told in many ways years before He came, sent to us to make things right, to show us we don't have to indulge even though we are in evils sight......that as children of God too we can strive to do as He, be Jesus like and loving as we can be......then like a lamb presented to God in that time and place, He laid His life on the alter and took our sins away......now whenever we find ourselves living the life of Sodom and Gomorrah, we can turn to the Living Lamb and ask forgiveness and its over......After He died He came back to show us He still lives, then He touched the hearts of his Disciples making them vessels to have the power to make miracles and forever in His name - give...... and so that's Christians' claim to fame, we make miracles in Jesus Christ name......so its the eve of the day we celebrate the birth of a man who forever carries our hurt, the symbol of love, and the only way to our God since the day of His birth..."

MUSIC IN ME

"I hear a piano, fingers floating across its keys, to the backdrop of drum beats creating a feeling so deep in me......gives me visions of the Archangel as he'd come, on a white dragon, thunderous horns uniting all Gods children in the body of One......then the strings come in so sweet, followed by my singing of an original song, titled 'He loves Me'......suddenly my voice starts to play games with the piano keys, showing my hood side as my body rocks to the drum beat.....I close with the support of the same horns that led the way for the King, high so high my voice reaches, so high it brings the audience to their feet...... as I close out with just me, and the piano in a classic ending..."

~ ~ ~

LOVE MESSENGER

"I'm the messenger you been looking for, the one that confirmed your next baby would be a boy......I'm the messenger that said please duck and roll to protect your heart, I said there is something that's hooking me to you so we'll never be apart......I'm the messenger you been looking for, the one that confirmed that there is something else in life worth so much more......I'm the messenger that said please come back home, home to the one that God assigned to be  your backbone……..I'm the messenger that said that love is the key, that it is the bridge that's going to bring you to me..."

~ ~ ~

PLANT THE SEED

"God's Word is like anything in life we do, you plant a seed and it will come back to you.....when it comes back its no longer just a seed, spoken word or hallowed thing, it comes back a living, breathing thing.....patience and faith is what's needed for both to take root, patience that the seed planted was  done correctly and will one day be as valuable as diamonds or loot.... faith that God's Word is something you can bet on, stand on and have no doubt to say, that one day you'll see the reward for doing it God's way……..God's way isn't easy for its the impossible dream, you may have to go it alone with just Him, battling through a sea of many men…..you may be let down, have to suffer from a thousand arrows and slings, but you plant the seed by doing what God and you had originally agreed…..the seed of trust that you will do every move in a way He would want you too……if you can do it - even if life smacks your hand and say don't do that……God's Word is like anything in life we do, you plant the seed and it will come back to you…"

~ ~ ~

DRESS LIKE A STAR

"What we wear is a reflection of who we are, you don't have to be rich to dress like a star…..you just need to have pride in how you look, be it sports wear or high fashion with a casual hook…..what you wear dictates how you walk, it can give you confidence and provide you with just the right spark……a spark that starts deep within the heart that provides you with the confidence to see, that fashion is what defines the person you want to be……I like my fashion to be casual but sharp, to be an example of what you will find when you look deep within my heart…..a heart that is simple but yet complex, one that says I'm up for any test......what we wear is a reflection of who we are, and up to today I can confidently say that you're the 'flyest' dresser I've seen thus far..."

~ ~ ~

REFLECTIONS

"If we take a little time to reflect, slow life down so we can look back, we will see what works and what didn't, giving us opportunity to discover the solution that is hidden......sometimes we go through life too fast, and as a result what's best for us never last, for we are living in the joy of the moment disregarding the idea of atonement......sometimes we are so into "self" we can't see beyond our own health, we don't see that we are all interconnected somehow if my brother is sick we all get no further than a lonely lil' mile.....we reject what helped us get to where we are, cause we think that wont make us THE shining bright star......but if we take a little time to reflect, we'll learned that God smiles on us when we help..... we learn we're rich when we have friendships, when we acknowledge who has helped us..."

~ ~ ~

NEVER QUESTIONED

"Always questioned my feelings for potential love interest in the past, I'd hang on to see in what direct it would go, if the feelings would last……but never have I yet to question what I feel from you, never wondered what the feeling could be cause what I felt was something brand new…..its hard to describe something deeper and stronger than you've ever felt, stronger than even a past love that kept a marriage together until he's untimely death……always questioned my feelings of a sexual nature whether it would be return or whether its true, but I never questioned the realness of what I feel for you…"

~ ~ ~

YOUR FRIEND

"Must be like a special day each day to be considered your friend, so loving, giving, creative and enlightening in every way……I bet you treat everyone as if they are a star, willing to go that extra mile no matter where in the world you are……with everything you've accomplished, its normal to think the world evolves around you, but to tell you the truth I think the world evolves around you too…"

~ ~ ~
MIRROR IMAGE

"You're amazing to me cause God is amazing for placing you in my life, through you He told me everything is going to be alright……I trust you cause I trust God's choice, I'm reminded of his Love every time I hear your voice……you are my world cause God means everything to me, it was He that created you in my image and opened my eyes to see…"

~ ~ ~
FUTURE IN YOUR EYES

"I saw a future where all men were free, contracts were outlawed as unconstitutional, prisons turned into colleges to recondition those in need……I saw a future where your Soul mates were known from birth, that energy connection seen by men, no more lost childhood sweethearts, one night stands, occasional sex partners - all relationships that would end in hurt……I saw a future where brother loved brother, humans helped those not able, there were no more stories like Cane and Able……I saw that in the future we all were considered rich and no one held you down, everyone was pushed forward and over until their wealth was found…"

~ ~ ~

GOD'S EYE

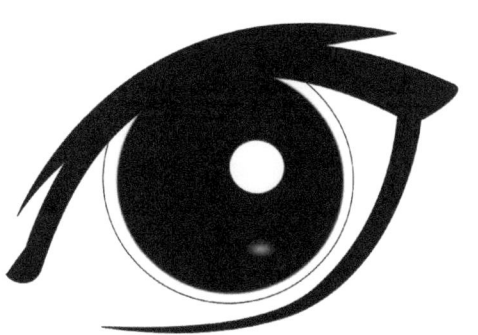

"Time has a way of passing you by, yet time is but a micro size concept to the mind's eye……time may distance some that you know, but yet it doesn't exist when love is what your waiting for……time heals wounds and un-sticks the glue that hold you two, yet it reminds one of the deepest of pains when there is someone you have to forgive and that someone is you……time is my friend it never passes me by, it doesn't exist for us two its the glue which holds me to you……time makes me smile from deep within, reminding me of my journey, tells me to regret nothing…… it calms my nerves when life tries to take things back, time is my friend and always has my back……time has a way of passing you by, yet time is but a micro thought in my God's eyes……time is what led me to you, time is

what we are depending on to make way for our truth…"
LOVE STORY

"The greatest love story ever told, that's what they will say one day……the girl who once wanted to be a nun, met the boy who had more girls than you could count - never one……20 years separated them by age they will say, but yet they were the same in every way……at first the world tried to keep them apart, until they learned that there was literally an invisible cord that connect their hearts……they started to see why you and me were meant to be, then the world turned to give their blessings to the making of 'we'……they then picked up the cause for us, started protecting and representing to the utmost for they know, that what's happening to us is the greatest love story ever told…"

~ ~ ~
IN YOUR EYES

"I love the way you love me, always something brand new, no gesture of love is the same, this is why I ask that you never, ever change……..I love

you just the way you are, an accumulation of experiences that are so familiar to me, I know you best - by far……I love the way your thoughts kiss mine in mid air, the way everyday you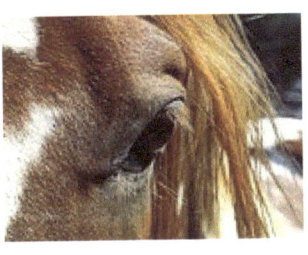
show me how much you truly care……A love so pure and true to others it seems odd, but to me my future was sealed when I saw in your eyes the face of God…"

~ ~ ~

FREEDOM'S FIGHT

"What would you do when faced with death, death cause you want freedom to be a man and not cattle together, fenced in, held down, would you
choose death, or would you choose the easy road of acceptance by giving up your freedoms for a easier way……what would you do when faced with scorn, scorn because you dare speak what only others whisper or refuse to even think, would you choose to be scorn, say what people want you to say, choose the easy way……what would you do when faced with suppression, suppression of your feelings of love cause its not approved by someone or another, would you choose to feel love for whomever you want, or would you let go of love

and choose the easy road to love self......I choose to face death and choose the hard way, speak out my mouth, I choose to be scorn so I could think what I believe God put in my heart, I choose love even though I knew the travels would be rocky, dirty and have many bandits attacking me in that land, but I did it knowing God approved and was pushing me forward to a day I dreamed - forever holding Love's hand..."

~ ~ ~

DANCE IT AWAY

"I'm seeing all the things I was raised on, good music, hopes and dreams, the thought of mind you can dance to achieving any- thing......in turn my kids grew with the same treasures as me, we sang away hate and danced around the ac- ceptance of emotional pains' weight......we danced and sang on cor- ners its true, laughed hunger and pain away for the arts was still in school......like slaves sing- ing in cottons fields in worship and praises, we had no time for self-petty our hopes were on a better day......I'm seeing all things of love cause that makes up what I be, so why wouldn't I believe and see that you wouldn't come back for me..."

~ ~ ~
SAVING HER

"I feed on you, as you feed on me, we keep each other full, we thirst for no more......I feel

like Joseph when he met the girl God had chosen......He had to believe what God had put in his heart, love this woman and to save her life you must depart......just think of how weird the moves he had to make seemed, I'm sure his family could not understand his thinking......but there came a day when the world finally knew what he did, think of the lessons made when he proved God was real and he wasn't so weird.....I'm sure they all started to see clearly as he, that God is amongst us now doing all sorts of miracles and special things......So I feed on you, as you feed on me as each other we carry, for I am to help you share your God given creativity - like Joseph helped Mary..."

~ ~ ~
MY HERO

"You're me now I can see, same style, same eyes, same desire to be......You're my hero and I'm yours I know, from the back, the front, constant protection, evident by the glow we create in our Souls'

affection...I do for you and don't expect anything in return, when you acknowledge it I blush cause it's something I never look for that's how I was learned……..you do for me not knowing whether I will ever see, you don't do it for you, you do it for me...You're me now I can see, same talents, same loves, same desire to be free..."

PATH OF CHRIST

"I love the Lord, but most of all I fear the Lord and respect what He says, cause He created life and He can take it away......not even Satan has that power, he thinks he does, that's cause God allows things to happen to us.......He gave us free will, free will of choice to learn and grow, see the result of our works good and bad, gave us the possibility of a life we thought we would never have......He allows us to choose worldly gains or the Heavenly gifts He has sent, they look the same but they are very, very different.....one gain benefits self in reality the benefactor is evil and the other gain benefits others, even if it takes away from us, the benefactor is our brothers......one road is easy everything seems to fall in ones lap and the other constant pitfalls, mountains to climb, rivers divide - you must tackle them all to get to that......all my life I've been the underdog because I've chosen the path of resistance that benefits others, that uplifts my brothers......I love the Lord, but most of all I respect his Words, for they are the blueprint to Heaven here on earth..."

~ ~ ~

LIVING WORDS

"They say if its meant to be it will come back again and again until what's meant to be is, they say no delays made by man can stop what's meant to be - just change how it will come to me.......that any disruption from God's path will be used to enhance what was meant to be your advance......they say if you have faith, as much as a mustard seed, that God's plan will happen and if you stay true to Him that all things will come to me - as He promised it will be......They say all who speak on His behalf are not really  His children, not the mouth piece of His Word and follow them you shouldn't......so I live as if His Words were alive, as if He was here right by my side....He is my pastor, my preacher, my mentor, the one I look up to and cherish......I consult him in everything I say and do, and because of it - He led me to you.......They say if its meant to be it will come back again and again until what's meant to be is, they say no man can stop what the Father has planned, no one can take what He lovingly gives......so in patience I wait and thank God every time you reach out to me, and praise His name when the messages from you - I can see..."

~ ~ ~

DREAMT A DREAM

"I feel like I'm living a dream, within a dream, one dreamt since the beginning of time that said you were mine......in the 2nd dream we are to take on a monumental task, so in the 1st we had to be schooled and live experiences to get answers to questions in the 2nd we might ask.......in the 2nd we will know our purpose clearly, which way to go, for its the 2nd that will change the world in which we know......I feel like I'm in transitioning for the 2nd that was already fore told, it's unreal watching it unfold, I feel like I'm winning the worlds most prestigious gold.......like years of physical training has amounted to this, what I've been preparing for, to conquer this very moment and live in bliss..."

~ ~ ~

KNOWING THE WAY

"I remember my first prayer when I found out what a prayer was, I asked God for wisdom so

I'd make the best decisions as I go through life - I just wanted to get it all, to get it all right......I know I had to have been under 5, but I already knew each moment of decisions

could cost me my life...... I've testified since then that my prayer came to be, I talk of the gift of wisdom my Lord He gave to me......when it comes its not of me though, the wisdom that comes is what I call God's flow.....He uses me as His vessel for all to see, that through His 'wisdom' He made me the best that I can be......we all have the power to channel God's flow, but first its just one thing He wants us to know......that there is nothing good and worth while in this life without Him, that He died so we can all begin again.......He wants us to walk in His shoes as Jesus Christ, without that walk, there is no eternal life..."

Journey To Love: A Book of Poems
By Eunice Moseley, MS, M.B.A.

Chapter II

Forbidden Friendship

Our friendship at this point has developed into a deep love and respect. We decide to "date," my generation would say we were "seriously talking." I am admiring his enthusianism for my emails and he is admiring my love for his art. He is becoming more sober looking on stage, the group is more sober looking. They are starting to do dance steps in sync again, growing more sharp in their stage presentation. Though still off retainer I am seeing my strategies being implemented and that they eventually got through to Oprah Winfrey; the playwright/movie producer; the movie distributor/producer; BET Network, L'Oreal, the cell company, and other "seeds" I planted that we were waiting for replies on.

I can see he is still under attack by reading the social media subtweet posts, it seems they have access to a lot of celebrity social media profiles or are hacking them. For they are being used to send hate filled messages. They also use pictures to send their hate, pictures that coincide with something in my private life to let me know they are watching, or coincide with Love's message to tease and hate on them. They try to make me jealous by suggesting he is still dating others, or try to scare me off saying he is gay, or that I am not .

really talking to him. He tells me through his celebrity friends profiles to just "Believe" - and I do

Shortly after this the Orioles marketing campaign was something like "Believe." Their new theme song is released and he is the singer on it. The songs' promotions picture was just of a woman's eyes. I took it as him saying yes its me talking to you, because at the E3 expo him and I had an eye lock stir. II wrote a poem about it, "In Your Eyes." I could not take my eyes off him, I think it was his likeness to my late husband. He could not look away from me either. In fact he was giving an interview at the time he was stirring in my eyes.

> **(April 17, 2012) Me to Love:**
> "Believe...I just saw the television advertising on (the film) Lucky, first think I saw was the word 'Believe'...I might be wrong but I 'believe' that's about us too :)...commercial made me cry lol...wanna see that one again...hope we have a happy ending too…"

He is still using his friends as a sort of Othello. A month after we started "dating" he finds out that one of his dates were with child - son. I mentioned how I would understand if he leaves me. I said a son needs to be raised by his father. He assured me we are still "talking" and to still 'believe' him. To wait for him to be free, I assume of the contract. I said I would wait.

When I found out he had a son, I thought about my late husbands dream. I wrote a poem "Living The Dream."

They have seem to have stop verbally attacking Love. I am now the sole target, but I read how Love take up for me.

One day I woke up feeling "fear" that he had made a "deal with the devil," which was my exact words in my morning email to him. This was before I found out about the "contract" he was locked in. In subtweet arguments on social media he is telling someone how under-handed they were with the contract. They in turn blamed him for not seeing their underhandedness. Blamed him (and his celebrity friends who are under the same type contract) for trusting them. I wrote a poem about the misuse of trust. This situation scares me, sounds like legal slavery. I start ending my emails with "be safe, come back to me."

(May 19, 2012) Me to Love:
"I am getting threats of 'murder' now...they say if they had a chance they will kill you...they say ...that if I can't have him nobody will. They tried to curse me with Bible quotes...they liked a video through your youtube...it played backwards like devil worshipers...I liked it so you can see..."

I later piece-together through the back and forth, and his messages that he may be under house-arrest too. He wanted me to know. I saw a post that said, "they caught me riding dirty, but I'm clean now." It made me wonder if he was set-up by someone who knew he was dirty.

He told me through a friend to wait no matter how long it took. I said again I would wait. Through his celebrity friends social media profiles, their movies, songs and music videos they tell his story.

We have discovered there is a energy that flows from him to me, from me to him. I call it our "love-flow." We've prove it to each other again and again. He said when he feels me it feels like he is on fire. I wrote a poem about it, Love's Energy."

I admitted I first felt it right after the E3 expo. The energy literally threw me against the wall - if you can believe it. I then saw him and heard him speak to me. I admitted it to him in an email that I felt him making love to someone while thinking of me. That I could actually feel it. I told him when it happened and asked why he was thinking of me while making love to someone else. He admitted the timing was true, and via a post shortly after a picture of him with his group was posted on my Facebook timeline with him wearing the same expression that was on his face that I saw in my mind - like he was confirming.

I believe he was thinking of me when his son was conceived (timing), and I believe him when he says that that was the last time he slept with the baby's mother.

> **(August 23, 2012) Me to Love:**
> "I keep laughing at a post I know is you...said he couldn't cheat anyway cause him and his girl was sharing the same building and she had 3D vision lol…"

We can reach out with the energy to feel each other whenever we want. I can feel his hands touch me and his mouth kiss me. He can feel mine the same way.

I tell him when I feel his energy its like big explosion as you would feel at the height of love making - the big "O" I told him.

I got a message from God one morning, I knew it was Him because I heard it over and over again in my head, to keep my eyes on Love. I found out later why God told me to keep my eyes on him and I was so glad that I did.

> **(June 3, 2012) Me to Love:**
> "The movie had Mary J in it!!!...with a grey streak in the front of her hair (like me)...she was running a strip club...movie had a Rock star with Tattoos and always with women (like you)..he falls in love with a journalist (like me)...I cried through the whole movie lol..."

At a point I can tell that whomever is verbally attacking me has run into some powerful money, Oprah Winfrey type money. This is because the attacks have moved off social media and has moved to every facet of the media industry just to verbally attack me.

The attacks start to escalate and the hacking as well. They must have control over content for more than him, his group and his celebrity friends but most major online media outlets' profiles, AOL and Huffington Post content, national commercials , and major networks content, such as CNN

Now who else in media has the money, power and influence to accomplish this throughout the media, but Oprah I am thinking. The person Love was waiting to hear from.

The one I can tell has been in contact with them, not only because his former dates, staff or business partners brag about Oprah being in control, but through pictures, news captions, and her magazine covers I can tell she is virtually watching me too. Someone with influence and connections years deep have inflamed this situation - financed it.

I can tell he is watching my back online and off, giving me encouraging words and supporting my clients and projects - as I am supporting his. I start to end my emails by calling him "my hero."

He doesn't let this stop him. I was covering an event at a club and my hand fell on the chest of a guy my height, I felt a chain. As I was leaving my heart told me that was Love. I emailed him to ask. Soon after his celebrity friends start appearing in pictures with their hand on their chest where mine was on this guy. I took it to mean, "yes, that was me."

He posted on his Instagram profile that he would be starring in his own reality show about him and his son, titled "SisQo Kid." I emailed him that even though I'm camera shy I would appear on it if he wanted - but no one else's show but his.

I said this because someone is bragging about a reality show of ex-girlfriends to Oprah's twitter account. Soon after, his Instagram post about his reality show was deleted.

In this chapter of *Journey to Love...*, titled "Forbidden Friendship," we hang on to each other while a full all-out strategic campaign to separate us is put into action..

HAVING MY BACK

"I'm so proud to be your lady, to have you watch my every step, some may think its intrusive, but I think its the best gift you've given me yet - knowing someone will be there always to have your back……I'm so proud to be the apple of your eye, to be appreciated so much so you never question why…..you never question why the love is there because you already know the answer, understand its bases, that's the way it works when you're so in tuned to a person you know the answer - you feel it in many places……I'm so proud to have you be considered my man, though you turned out to be more than I had planned, but I'm proud cause you have shown me how I helped you to find the man you are today, a man that will never again loose his way…"

~ ~ ~
PROUD OF YOU

"When you are proud that others love what you love it's a testament that your taste is on target and your feelings are not wasted, that your choice ran true on all of its bases……when what you love is returned with the same or more intensity and pride, it's proof that the love is mutual that its real, deep deep down inside......not often will you find a love that can hang on so true, take a beating and keep on ticking, swim the deep oceans' blue, just to get to me so that I can forever love you......when you are proud that others respect what you love it mirrors their love for you, it proves that love is the key and love is Heaven sent, when others respect your choice and give you their blessing..."

~ ~ ~

PROUD WOMAN

"Every minute in your life can be a turning point, that's why each step is to be contemplated and each word given much thought......each greeting felt a 1,000 times over, each decision another layer securely woven......I've said it once and I will say it again, no decision, step or word spoken am I regretting......for each one, whether it brought me pleasure or not in any way, has made me the woman I am so proud of on this very day..."

~ ~ ~

WARRIOR FOR LOVE

"I decided long ago as a baby only 5 years old, that if there is a choice to love or hate I choose love for Heaven's sake......I decided that if Jesus could die for me in love, then I could at least live in the same vein and with that mind-set it changed who I am......I became a warrior for Love demanding nothing less, my symbol became the dove and when it came to upholding peace - I out stood the test......I decided long ago as a wife to a black man society was determined to kill from afar, that I would always honor that population that had no clue about the depth of their own scares......a population oppressed from the start, jailed and treated like girls by those afraid that collectively they could probably rule the world......I decided long ago at the age of 16 that if I ever find a black man who would be true to me and make me his world, that I would give him my heart and Soul and forever be his girl..."

~ ~ ~

TAKE A DIVE

"To love someone from a far and trust they are the person they say they are is a testament to your measurement of faith, to give your heart up in many ways……to communicate on a different level no words, body movements, eyes or hands, where many can guess at the message but only one can really understand……to take a dive when everyone is saying 'don't jump,' nothing driving you on but a feeling and what was seen in a look from one……to love someone to this degree it can be, for this love has happened several times to me…"

~ ~ ~

YOUR HAND

"When I need strength cause my body says I can't, I look for help and suddenly I see your hand……fingers long and thin, perfect for playing piano, physically strong able to keep me holding on…..when I need love cause negativity is taking its toll, I remember feeling your love-flow and realize that's my wealth - the feeling is like pure gold……when there's no one around to make me laugh out loud, I see your sweet messages and they put - on me - a big smile…….some messages offer wisdom, some funny, some with knowledge I've never heard, some with warnings to hold, just hold on …….when I need strength cause my body says not now, I think of your lifestyle how you keep going and suddenly the energy I need is found…"

~ ~ ~

ENERGY OF CHRIST IN ME

"Nothing can compare to the love we share, only few make it through, takes someone who'd just push, just push his way right on in - like you…….knew he'd have a passion for who I am, hang on to me cause I'd do the same…….knew he'd ignite my inner flame, I'd look at him and see who I am……nothing can compare to the energy we share, if we could bottle it the world would be a better place - no aggression anywhere……the good feelings from that energy, we'd give it out for free, for the energy we make is what's call 'Christ within me'…"

~ ~ ~

CRAVING YOU

"I crave to eat you like sweet candy, my favorite thing to consume.....when I'm thirsty I turn you into a drink, an ever lasting flowing stream......my appetite is satisfied with just a glimpse of your face, for I have a gift where I'm able to take of you a taste......that's why I crave to eat you like red velvet cake, mixed with whip cream filling in a very special place..."

~ ~ ~

OCEAN DEEP

"My love runs deep, deeper than any stream can reach......can't think of how much I would endure, thoughts of it too deep runs to the core.....can't feel the entirety of your love for me it's too much runs entirely too deep......when I focus on the magnitude of it, it's hard to believe that someone of your caliber would even notice me......the invisible girl living in an entirely different world......not many like me they see, but because of the depth of your love suddenly all eyes on me..."

~ ~ ~

CREATIVITY DEEP

"Creativity takes the normal and makes it unique, leaving a branding that says this belongs to me……many will try to imitate and perfect, but no one can really copy what God placed in your head…… creativity can come from anything, a sound, a look, words, the way someone sings ……when I dance I let my body do its thing, everyday I write poetry, the next day I may sing '…… creativity, I was born with it, it's who I am but one day I had to suppress it, life just saw it as kiddy's games and didn't make time for it…… don't see that creativity is the biggest industry in the world, society treats it like a dumb blond with curls…..but meeting you has awaken the creativity deep within, it's been like Heaven to see my old creative friend again..."

~ ~ ~

CONVERSATION WITH GOD

"When every ones gone and you're all alone, its just you and God talking about - in life - what you have done…..He'll see through it all that I let love be my gift that represents me: that I am smile, laughter, hope, one known for giving a gentle push in the right direction for the dope……He'll see I picked up sword to protect the weak and disadvantaged out of love, expecting no return, one not known to attack but to defend until His war is won by the return of His only begotten Son……He'll see through it all you have grown into a man with a heart of gold: one that gives, that encourages, that catches the weak when they fall and protects His commandments of age old……He'll see you went to the corners of the earth in search for freedom to be able to pick your own girl and He'll see when you found her, you did everything you could think of to tell her she's your world……when every ones gone and you're all alone, it's just you and God talking about what you've done, I hope meeting me was a favorable one…"

~ ~ ~

HUNGER TO LEARN

"I always had the hunger to learn, though there is nothing new under the sun, truth is nothing stays the same as life happens over and over again......so we adapt is how I see it, learning a new way to do things, learning that things are never how they seem - that's why my mind is always hungry to know new things......but the mind says everything that comes my way is not real enough to stay, I've learned too separate the BS from the truth - a skill some haven't learned how yet to do......I always had the hunger too - for fun, laughter and smiles the kind that turns enemies into one - one team, one thought, one friend, one heart......so to adapt to keep fun in my life, I try to keep my thoughts on what's true and that is the love I seem to continuously get from you..."

~ ~ ~

DESTINATION

"I hear planes off in the distance, destination unknown to me, but I know they took off with God's unconditional loving speed......I hear life just the same, as it makes for us a way......like a symphony that clicks with sounds' always leaving you wanting more, each day for us is a musical, the "Voyage to Love" tour......this musical sound can go from climax to sizzle always an emotional ride, but a joy when it's with someone willing to ride the tide......life is a wondrous magic called love, each day we reach out for it, never getting enough....now my symphony has changed its tune, as all eyes and ears turn to you..."

~ ~ ~
IN MY FRAME

"Always knew there was something about you, felt like home - just what was unknown.....so I kept you close in a frame with a note, that you belong in a group who I could turn to for hope......an example of a life that gave 100% to his craft, who saw a dream and followed straight to world class......a dream-stream that led to what you wanted to achieve, and so I did it too - two times, maybe three......I always knew there was something about you, found out what, with all of your clues - that you held a deep love for me, as I have held for you..."

LOVE SOLDIERS

"You've taken me on a journey, journey to lovers lane, you knew I would follow when you took my hand…..on the way you came under attack and my immediate instinct was to fight back…..I was double teamed as a result, but somehow you found a way to protect us from the back and from the front - and it seems you did it very well as far as I can tell……we continued on our journey and realized we weren't alone, life gave us another - made from part of your bone……
together we continued down the lane as planned picking up soldiers of love, the tried and true kind - heart of a lion and Soul of a dove…..you've taken me on a journey, journey of transformation, for the journey was to allow us to shed some things that got in the way of us for filling the desires of the Son - gathering His army so His battles can be won…"

~ ~ ~

HEART DANCE

"You take my hand and dance me round, sometimes in song, sometimes in your arms…until now its been in your heart, where only we can see, but being the man you are I think that's the best place to be……in a world where men are raw, the woman pool overflowing with too many to choose, to have a home in your heart is a clear sign your love for me is true……when that day comes when I can dance with you on the floor, it will be a natural flow as if we've lived it before……you take me with your love-flow from level 1 to 4 straight to the top, with just a thought powerful it knocked me completely out…… when the day comes when its physical in every way make sure we're alone on an island, for I will be roaring louder than a lion."

~ ~ ~

FROM HIS HAND TO HIS PLAN

"I wonder what was the plan 21 years after the birth of a man, to say lets do it again make another one, switch them during November - one comes Home and to the other its his birth month, this time give him a son and make him the father image of another one…….how will this play out in history, has to be a reason for it all, one that we just can't  see…... I wonder what was the plan that September when it all began, it put into motion a bond that the worlds' elite and powerful would look upon again and again…..they see a planned meet before time, a continuation of a circle come back until love it finds……I wonder what was the plan when God touched a little girl's hand, said you'll see things differently but don't fear I'm always with you since time began…. I'll send you someone who will understand, cause when he was a boy I touched his hand……you see, you are the key that brings His love to me…."

YOUR FLAVOR WANTING MORE

"There is so many dimensions to you it's crazy, like hundreds of different popcorn flavors…… each one as delicious as the next, yet they don't add on any pounds to your waist - just leaves you with that sweet wanting more and more taste…… that's your love so far to me, each day a new flavor that you release, each act of love is sweeter than the first - as if you wake up with the 'me' thirst…….there is so many dimensions to me its crazy, think you seen all I can give, you've just seen the gravy…"

ETERNITY'S PAGES

"There is nothing new under the sun, everything has a beginning that started with just one……one thought that has been thought of before, the difference is God allows us to visualize how to open that particular door……one sound heard for an eternity, repeated by different voices and heard by different ears……we say to ourselves why didn't I think or sound like that, that's because God kept the desire under His hat throughout the years……

He wants us to appreciate the purpose of the sound, the gravity of the thought, He wants us to understand what it is we're looking for, so we're satisfied, and wanting no more……there is nothing new under the sun, that includes our love, becoming as one…... the kind that last throughout the ages, striving always to be one with no fears on eternity's pages…"

~ ~ ~

LOVE, GOD'S ENERGY

"At the end Love will win, if you study history enough you will see that everything begins and ends with love for it is God's energy……who in their right mind thinks they can beat God and His Holy plans……we think we've won, think we've planned, think we've gotten over but in the end its still 'gonna' be God's plan cause He is the Man……this life is all about Him, it begins and ends with Him no matter how long we fuss and cuss, we're just here living like a squirrel trying get a nut……at the end Love will win you see, if you study history the giving of love, protection of love and cultivation of love is life's only problem solving key…"

~ ~ ~

LOVE SURROUNDING ME

"You see what I see before I see it, I feel what you're going to go through before you go through it……I wonder if what you see is as clear as when I see you, it's like a projection that if I reached out my hand would just go right through……I wonder if what I feel of things to come for you is because my love is surrounding and protecting you……you see what I see before I see it, I appreciate and need it…… hope love is surrounding and protecting you, I hope it gives you strength when you need to push and kick your way through…"

~ ~ ~

THE MEET

"You have to ask yourself why is the meeting of two such as catastrophic event, that a team is assembled to prevent it…… both have a history where people say, 'such a sweetie,' but yet forces move to make sure their image is damage so much so they desire no meeting……you have to ask yourself why people project their wants and dreams on others, and your wants and dreams they take or try to smother……if it makes you happy, but doesn't satisfy their measurement of success, they label you a failure, try to take away what you have until there is nothing left……you have to ask yourself why people take things personally, most things not meant for them at all, or not meant for them to hear, then they work it so its justification to 'attempt' to make your life a mess, create an atmosphere of fear……but what was meant to be back in 1996 will come back round to me as intended, cause we both wont rest until that day I'm next to you breathing…"

SMILE BACK

"I love when people smile, it's like sunshine, the kind that makes you lift your head up to meet its ray - a smile can really make a person's day……I love to smile, in fact, it's who I truly am in every way - fun and happy-go-lucky is how I frame each day……I love your smile, big and bright, you should do it more often as you conquer the night……remember as you go about starting from scratch, take time for the little things and remember to give a smile back…"

~ ~ ~

LOVE CLOCK STILL CLICKING

"Clock ticks as life ticks the right mix to fix itself for another day…each second it beats as the heart beats to carry life's flow along its way……each day you've never missed a beat, answered all my questions, as far as I can see……amazing how my Love you still clickin' that life beat - with me…"

~ ~ ~

OLD STORY

"So it goes same old story, lovers meet, depart and search the world for that day they can get another chance to say 'for you my love is deep, here, I'm yours eternally to keep'……but life's a b*tch, throws up a wrench, test the limits of what you claim you're giving……no one believes it could end well, for once in their lives that pool turned into a dry well……but to their surprise - not mine or yours - we prove the love will surely endure……so it goes same old story history books' hold that when your glass' is 1/2 full you'll always reach your goal…"

~ ~ ~

TAKE 'ME' TIME

"As a loner one thing I learned in life to be true, the ground won't open up if you don't give away or rent out the space in front of you……you don't have to answer when there's a knock at the door, or be subjected to anything that doesn't make you feel the love of the Lord…"

LOVE, MY SHADOW

"My shadow follows me or so it seems, but I say my shadow is in front of me, all around, no matter what direction I might be……always there to show me the position of the sun, so that I may face the world clearly however it may come……you're my shadow always there, doing everything in your power in ways 'I' know you care……my shadow follows me and now I know, he'll stay with me no matter where I go…"

~ ~ ~

LOVE WATCHES MY BACK

"You watch my back and I will watch yours, an old familiar road we been down before……I'll listen when you talk even if you don't have much to say, and each time you leave my side, my heart will go with you as you go about your day…"

~ ~ ~

YOUR LOVE IS LIKE HOT TEA

"I make sure my life is like tea, more than its substance, heated just right for me... …just enough energy dipped until it visually puts a smile on my face, sweeten just right with the people money can't replace……even if I drink the cup when its cooled, my tea is still 'gonna' be tasting so very good…… especially since my life served up you, you help melt away the harshness like hot tea melts away the morning dew…."

~ ~ ~

LOVE, LIKE THE FLOW OF MUSIC

"I love it when music flows from you to me, it's like I'm a puppet and you pull the strings…..to give control I'll take the chance, for all you want your puppet to do is dance……I hear melodies I've never heard before and I wonder did I create this or is this him taking me into his world……suddenly I have no control when the music takes over my Soul……I be feeling like my voice can hit the Heavens, the vocal power multiplies, more clear, silky smooth like the best days are coming for me and you…… when I'm in your zone my heart aches to sing originals songs made just for me, deep ballads that go long…… just think Love, when that day comes the vocals you will inspire in me through your songs, the things you'll have my voice do like holding the notes so long…… you will find the right songs to fit my voice and what it can do, when your music finally starts to flow from me to you…"

~ ~ ~

LET GOD DRIVE LOVE

"God gives us want we need, in the order in which we need it to please……it's hard for us to see that in every negative there is a plus, and that only He can see what's a head of us……if we're wise and truly lovers of peace, we'll let God drive and take the back seat……our GPS system will take us down the wrong road, run us right into a brick wall, but his guidance system takes a wrong road and makes it right, and blows a door through a wall that was once closed tight……God knows the truth in all its glory and shame, He knows who is real and who is playing games……when we cover up the truth in order to please, at the end of the day God allows the lie to knock us to our knees…….sometimes that doesn't mean you become broke and financially poor, doesn't have to mean no one is willing to open any doors……sometimes it means having to see yourself in a reflection that's not so nice, and the reality of what you see is what makes you drop to your knees……it's at that point that you will find, the truth comes with a bodyguard that's with you all the time…"

~ ~ ~

LOVE, THE UNEXPLAINABLE

"How can you explain the unexplainable, to describe a feeling that words can't explain, some try and the words are not what they mean, some do but others reactions say its not what it seems……love is the substance that words can't begin to imitate, when it's felt to a depth that allows Souls to meld into one face……a face that when you look you see yourself, a love like that is more valuable than monetary wealth…..it's a substance that as long as the passion is there, the energy will forever exist as a sign that you care…… the one thing about love - in its many forms and sizes - is that even after one leaves the bond, love still carries on…… love is still there held by the other following behind them in thought and in prayer, forever existing as a sign that you once cared……I know these facts to be true, for in the few relations I've had, the love has endured - as it will with you……we gravitate to what we know is true, what's good for one, may not be good for you..."

AGAINST THE TIDE

"In life we are always swimming against the tide, always fighting since birth just to stay alive……as children we relied on our parents to make sure we survived, to think some kids have to do it alone never knowing why……so they grow up thinking every man for themselves, so stepping on a friend is just what it takes to get to money's wealth……they were never taught that wealth is a parents love, the kind that's always there when everyone else gives up…..all they know is fore filling their own needs, they were never taught to others please……so in life when you're swimming against the tide, just know you'll get there but it may take a while…... know God has control so hang on to a rock, and then let the tide just ride, just ride it on out…"

~ ~ ~

TOUGHEN UP FOR LOVE

"Pieces of our lives make up who we are, it holds on to the real, it gives pieces it takes, my life in comparison to others has been such a piece of cake……hardships, yes and we didn't have much, but as a kid that I didn't see, all I saw was the love……in return I learned to love, every decision to take me towards that sweet peaceful dove…… it even became a hindrance - until the Navy toughened me

up…..that experience said, 'no matter what comes you can defeat it, harden up and God will give you what's needed'……so as the pieces of my life falls into place, I'm just glad it has allowed me to stay strong enough to once again see your face…"

~ ~ ~

LOVE, A SHOOTING STAR

"Funny how different yet how a like we are, you raised on stages and me appointments here and there in my car……though you keep one foot hanging in your business and the other deep in the creative process, mine is deep in the process of business, with my Soul full of the creative essence……it's ying and yang, melting together in a different sought of way, its like night falling in love with day…..its like lyrics finding a rhythm with beats, its like what good music does to a person's feet……funny how different yet how a like we are, I'm your Navy anchor and you're my shooting star…"

~ ~ ~

LOVE, INVISIBLE ENERGY

"Takes my breath away when that fire hits me, invisible energy targeted right at me…… focused in its mark, no time for talk, that love flow just wants to go deep, determined to weld itself onto me…"

LOVE, DO-OR-DIE

"What fun to come for you and I, going through life bringing the party to each others smile…..loving each move, sound and notion that the other makes……always striving to give, not worrying about the  take……sometimes I wonder what I'd do if the roles were reverse, would I let the hype of my industry pull me away until I'm not even sure if you ever were……what would make you so important that I'd keep communication lines open, that I'd enlist all my friends to hold the door open……I'd say it was the open attention you give online, right down to the look in your very familiar eyes, it was the devotion and passion to always be by……yes, what fun to come for you and I, two people Heaven put together to show a relationship can be 100% - do-or-die…"

~ ~ ~

LOVE GIVES SECOND CHANCES

"Each day when you wake and open your eyes to seek and find, is another chance to reach your goals - to touch another's life and watch beauty unfold…..It's another opportunity to seek love if its out of reach, to mend bridges you've burnt cause you were too weak to keep……It's another chance to change your plans and try reaching your goals in another way, another chance to seek love's light to brighten up a darken way……each day I wake and find out that you are still here with me, I pitch myself to make sure I'm not in a dream……I guess it's the same for you, each day discovering how deep my love reaches - new evidence that my love is true……if I am to you what I feel I am, then it's another day to give thanks for the hook-up arranged by The Man…"

~ ~ ~

SAID AND DONE

"When it's all said and done, we've survived more battles than we've won……we've changed into someone we're proud of as we react to the people and the world around us…… we've completed our search for that one person that understands and completes us……we've nurtured young lives that grew to be decent human beings, people that in some way changed the world too and left positive feelings to be felt by me and you……we've loved our family enough that it comforts them when we're gone, that they speak of us often, like an old classic song…….when it's all said and done, we will have touched hearts more than we've won, and that touch put a smile on the face of our Heavenly Father and His Son…"

~ ~ ~

STANDING OVATION

"When all spotlights fade away there's no money no fame no chances of gain no words to be said no battles to be won, my Love I will still be here all eyes on you with a standing ovation…"

~ ~ ~

LOVE, ARCHANGEL ON HIS DRAGON

'There's nothing more precious than love, there's something sweet about it, soft like a baby's skin, the smell and feel like everyday is a new beginning…… there's nothing more stronger than love, can withstand all substances, and keep on kicking, no there's nothing more precious than love how it makes you wanna sing with the passion and power of ten……I see you in everything I do, so glad life showed me you…… the moment I saw you in your cap, the way the brim hides your eyes, I said, how precious is that…… there's nothing more precious than love, builds self esteem, when you're loved for self and not for things……I see the world changing for the good for that's how we two roll in the hood…… I see it changing now Love, Archangel on his dragon - can hear and I hope that means - you're almost home you're almost here…"

~ ~ ~

ONLY LOVE ENTERS HERE

"My world is that of peace, try to enter with anything other, you get the sweep……my minds on laugher, jokes and uplifting at the utmost, you take me wrong, then we must be listening to two different songs……My world sees greatness in small things, beauty in a kiss, I notice the morning dew, a butterfly's kiss……money gained don't impress me none, for it goes as fast as it comes - not to mention, life's a bit*h……, I've had plenty money more times than once……what I know is at any level I will eat, got too many that love me so in my world that helps me sleep……my hearts on forgiveness, finding love in everything, if that's not what your talking, then I'm just not listening…… In my world all things bring a smile, I see the good in most, but to the evil it discovers - I 'ain't' no joke……try to bring confusion to my world and you won't get far, cause everybody in my world is a superstar…"

FLAMES OF LOVE GO DEEP

"Feeling you deep within, so deep - flames still burning......felt you last night through every part of me, as if you were rocking me to sleep......I remember thinking as I faded into the deep, what your love has gone through cause of me......someone on the other side of the track, one willing to have your back......one not living within the frame of what some call the winning game......but we know a winner we are, the day we decided to give each other our hearts......we're winners cause we feel it deep within, so deep years later its still deeply burnin'…..burning with nothing more than a memory and a energy bond, felt deep below and birth in a song..."

~ ~ ~

LOVE THEY CLAIM

"When passions of love are involved there is no telling, we can train our bodies to do unbelievable things, but what you do with love - it has no limits……nothing agitates a hater but to see God in two people in love, looking and feeling happy with the glow of the Heavens up above…..that's my experience which is how I learned to duck-and-roll, while holding fast to love the ultimate gold……the gold is a relationship that makes you complete, that replaces your weaknesses and uplifts you to where you need to be…..one filled with laughter, respect - see I know it's true - that its possible to have one when the love is true…… when passions of love are involved, you can forget building walls, locking doors, spreading lies to kill the vibe, you - and those around you - once love is ignited, is never the same, when two people take that dive and love they claim…"

~ ~ ~

LOVE HOLDS YOU

"They say God don't give you more than you can handle, that He knows what you are capable of and softens any falls with His love…… that's real love when you think about it for a minute, it test you to the limits, it knows, it holds your soul, and it takes care of you like your solid gold……it spoils you, but still allows you pain by giving you your choice so knowledge you will gain……,but through all these ups and downs real love knows only one thing, that the one that holds you in their heart is worth risking everything……that's what God wants His children to do, risk it all to say 'I love you'…"

MUSIC IN ME

"When it comes to love it's not hard to see, there is love in the world in every part of the land, the hills and the seas......love is that which makes you smile, its what makes it home, when you haven't been there in a while, the place always full of fun......it's what keeps that passion light burning, gives you energy, the hunger for learning, longing to be free......when it comes to love it's not hard to see, that I will always have love as long as the music is in Me…"

~ ~ ~

WHAT FEEDS THE SOUL

"I know a place where all men go, to search for truth that feeds their Souls......some search in the shadows of others' feet, some search the waters so blue so deep......most take a lifetime searching through crowds, a forest of people rooted in their own beliefs......they search in clubs or while jogging in the park, then one day they discover what they're seeking is in the heart......they learn that their journey has been spent trying be the one that 'wins,' then discovering they've won the wrong somethin'......for I know a place where all men go in search of the truth that would feed their Souls, its warm and loving and never cold……in everyone's journey there's a time they discover that what they seek they can not meet, until they love that other side of what they call 'me'…"

~ ~ ~

WHEN LOVE IS REAL

"Sometimes it's not love for someone that holds us back, it's the rejection, a non-understanding of why someone would do that……it's internalized and taken personal - seen as bad, but when your self esteem is high you externalize it and say well they'll miss the best thing they never had……my experiences have taught me when love is real, there is no rejection when love you still feel……as long as the love is returned with as much passion as it's given, no matter what is said or done that love it just keeps going on and on……sometimes it's not the love that keeps us holding strong, it's that inner voice that says when you love - you can't go wrong……what good is it to hold on to love that's not real, it's like driving a car with a second wheel….you want to drive one way and they the other, and at the end of the day you've gotten no further……so I'm looking for someone who knows how to drive, wheel and deal, someone with a love I can not only see but one I can

feel……
when that
person is
brought
to me by
life, the
test will
be if he

makes me his wife…"

~ ~ ~
JOURNEY TO LOVE

"Once, I saw the
entirety of your
life go by in your
eyes, it was so un-
believable I could-
n't take my eyes
away I can't
lie……there were
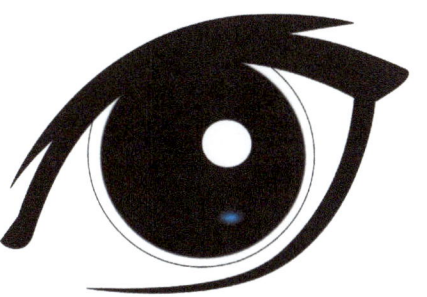
parts that made me smile and parts that took my
breath away, parts that made me cry……it only
took a minute, two at the most but that was all that
I needed to see my dreams and my hopes- the ex-
perience was so dope……then as quickly as it be-
gan the spell was broken and then the 'journey' to
Love began…"

~ ~ ~
LOVE, COMES TO ME

"As you go about your day, making life grand
along the way, you take the time to check on me,

see if I'm ok, what it is I see……if what I see is meant to hurt or based on a lie, you give that back to me void of hate covered with your smile…….every now
and then when you are in need, you stop your world and come to me……I feel you now, your body is callin' me, I feel like dropping everything to attend to your needs……so as you go about your day, making musical masterpieces, know that my body is alert and ready to please…"

~ ~ ~
BOOTCAMP

"Boot camp taught me many things I never knew, thought if my brother and sister
could do it, I could do it too….it taught me physically I could train my body to do anything - and here's why, we are physically limited only by what our brains think we're not…..I learned there is always a leader and followers in a group, that we are beyond race, religion and even personalities - we're one too…….we are Souls with a purpose at any given time - good or bad - that we all struggle

to hold on to that which makes us happy let go of what makes us sad……we were so far from home away from those that loved us even when we're bad, I saw many couples began mating in search of a love like that……as I watched people from every part of the world try to exist in peace, I learned during boot camp that the love they seek lived within me……Navy boot camp taught me many things I never knew before, how small the world is when one person is left with only themselves to give, only themselves to adore…."

~ ~ ~

SPEED OF LIFE

"Sometimes it's like the world is going so fast, running at the speed of life and all I can see is streaks of yellow, red and blue lights……then out of the maze I see your face, with a look in your eyes that can't be replaced……a look it seems people would kill for, blind to the fact that I'm the only one that holds the key to that door……at the same time, you see my face in the maze, and immediately thank God for the day…… but no sooner than you see my face, life violently takes me away…… stunned and unsure if what I saw was real, I hold on to the lighthouse, hoping to see your face again…….all through your journey as life passes you by, you plan for the day you'll get to see my smile…….so you search and search, I hold on tight waiting to see, 'til next we meet and in my mind I hear you speak, next time Love - you'll never get that far away from me...."

~ ~ ~

IDENTICAL SOULS

"What a delight it is for me to know that someone is almost identical to my Soul...... never will I feel unique in the sense, that I wonder what this thing called life is, for me, meant...... I could go on with life without ever greeting your face, and I'd still be able to say that meeting you wasn't a mistake......He introduced me to a world I never knew was there, a world he knew would scrutinize, but he knew I wouldn't fail......what a delight it has been to know that someone knows me that well, he knows what I'm capable of even before I myself can tell..."

~ ~ ~

THE HONORABLE THING

"Some times in life its best to give credit where credit is due, for nothing in life is accomplish with just you...... there were so many

times in life others' success was based on my work, sweat and tears, where most people who witnessed this got upset that the credit wasn't shared......I never did, cause I knew what I did before I could do again and their good fortunes based on my work would soon come to an end.......truth is I'm not the person to go around bragging I did this and I did that, I just always thought the honorable thing would be to - at least - give those that help you a pat on the back.......a follow through on a promise to share the benefits or give a tip, and then far as I'm concern you can have all the credit...."

~ ~ ~

A MAN'S PLACE

"When life tries to drive you insane, you just keep your eyes on 'The Man'.....His love and light puts a smile on any face that takes the time to live in His grace......it's hard for some women to give men the drivers seat, too many generations of men of women they mistreat....so slowly women took control, began to drive and many just left men behind......but in their hast to take man's place, they left behind those with a gentleman's taste......my experience has shown me instead of taking control by driv-

ing when he's weak, let him do his thing and gently give directions from the back seat……for even if he is not fully in control its best to keep the roles as God see's fit and work as a team, cause in the long run its so much better for your man's self-esteem…."

~ ~ ~

INSIDE OF ME

"Sometimes I feel you inside of me like the movie The Matrix when The One entered the enemies body, sometimes I feel you inside me, not beside me, but as if we are one……don't think anyone would believe me if I tried to explain, it's like trying to explain my pain……people only see what they see, how do you explain something that's inside of me….that's where faith and a person's credibility comes into play, you believe them without further explanation - have faith in what they say……my reputation, I'm told, holds that credibility what people hear from me they tend to believe…….but even those when I told of our story, of the feelings I hold, they didn't believe me for it seemed too much like magic - too unbelievable to be sold…"

~ ~ ~

TO HOLD THE GOLD

"They say nothing worth having comes easy, I knew this early in life believe me……it was why I took on at 17 the responsibility of a business, where grown people had to depend on me - I took on a life that was so busy……yes it was hard to get up earlier than most my age and get home, oh so very very late……but I knew one day that experience might help me at my next step in life, to join the Navy, help my country fight……it was when my commander said to the room, 'who here has supervised, don't mind getting up before dawn?' I was the only one - so at 19 I became manager of the Internet communications between the Navy and the Pentagon……that experience helped me in civilian life, gave me a job where I was one of the highest paid - I saw no financial strife…… and in college it gave me the organization skills I needed while producing TV, radio and stage, and the professional character I developed led to some internships that were paid…..that undergrad college journey was hard, my learning disadvantage kept pushing me back to the start…… I did it in 6 when others did it in 4, but when I was done I was qualified to walk through opportunities' door……so through the last 6 years of graduate school financial struggles that

I've had to endure on my way to my goal, I think of everything I've been through and remember I WILL one day hold the gold and much much more...."

~ ~ ~

DANCING PARTNER

"If we were performing partners imagine what they'd see....see your hand reach out for me to hold that left one, as you tell me you're on your way

home.....imagine you on stage and then suddenly I appear, your dancing partner, face hidden with the rim of a fedora oh so fierce......we'd change into our favorite characters at will, a reminder of how we met playing roles the audience will never forget.....my character with long legs, big boobs and lips big enough to paint a portrait...... I'd have a stomach so small, women would think I was a doll.....your character with a broad chest, legs of steel, lips big as mine, so juicy kissing brings no regret......we'd have the height of giants from the land of Oz everyone would think you were 10 feet tall....if we were performing partners imagine what they'd see.....my hand reaching out across the stars, to hold you when I missed a beat…"

~ ~ ~

A MIRACLE

"They say God takes a mess and makes a miracle, I believe He does that to show that He is in control and our futures only He can hold......sometimes in life as it passes by, we get catch up in the happenings as we wonder just how.....is it manipulation? desire? or maybe a natural characteristic that says your not a leader but you are a follower.... we follow cause we don't want to take control, we get in a position where we feel we must please the entire world....strong is the man/woman who can still be an individual in a crowd, to simply make an awesome God proud.....sometimes that takes courage in a way that only He can see, when man can't understand what's happenin'......He allows us to make decisions that create a mess in hopes that we learn next time to not second-guess......so far there isn't a decision I've made when it comes to you that I regret,

I see that its worked to your benefit, therefore I've passed the test...... and if I had to do it all over again - there would be no tossing and turning, or losing sleep cause I'd know as a result in the end, you'd finally win...... and I, through your eyes, would be able to see how small the world is, how we all contribute to life's very existence to just be...... to see how deep a man's love for a woman can take him, how for the one he loves he'd do just about anything......to see you literally go to the ends of the world using your clout, so therefore of your love I just don't have a doubt..."

~ ~ ~

I LOVE YOU MORE

"In reality I love you more than you know, that's what you say, that's what I pray......cause I have faith in your abilities and your love for me shows you care, that's why I'd follow you anywhere.....I'd follow you even into the dark and not fear any man, as long as you're with me, holding my hand...... I prayed for your team I remember the day, cause I know in business you can't make it any other way......I can feel when you're around those you trust, there's nothing like that

feeling man, the energy from it makes me want to dance, dance, dance.......and even though I couldn't be there during the climb, thanks to that energy that I share with you, I was there during every step, every day - anyway......so when you say you love me more than I know, I say to you - ditto..."

~ ~ ~

LOOKS LIKE HOME

"Your hands look like home, every line a road I traveled on...... the shape, the length, I've seen before, evidence of a man who uses his art to endure......hands that are perfectly made to carry your babies and I'm sure, hands that can be expertly use as a woman-allure......your hands long to hold me it's clear to see and I can feel, that your hands they belong to me......I wonder do my hands look like home to you, would you know them, have you traveled my road too.....one of my hands has a life of its own, I often wonder to whom it belongs..... the power behind it I always thought was too much for a woman but then, that was the hand that helped me in life to discipline.....when I look at it now I'm reminded that I found the truth, that one of my hands it belongs to you...."

~ ~ ~

LOVE NATURE

"I love nature in everyway, love watching it as it goes about its day......from the butterfly so gentle yet able to hang on during a big wind, the birds singing of found food and the coming of a warm morning......the bees searching here and there for the taste of something sweet, the wind blowing the trees, adding sound to the silence......bees ever so silent as they transport the fertilizing power of the pollinate......colorful flowers of so many kinds, blossoming and folding depending on the time......our love-flow-energy is also nature in its proper place, it travels through mountains, time and space...... it skips over people, pass through clouds, hovering over brooks to get to its place, that Love that it found that's evident on our face......what a wondrous gift God gave when He made nature in its detail, there is no doubt believing in The Maker of this, with Him we can not fail..."

~ ~ ~

COMMUNICATION

"Imagine couples seeing what their partner sees like you and me, there would be less and less number of divorces for communication is the key.......when they are separated they are literally still there never apart, always along for the ride, a passenger of the heart.....and  like me, literally, I know and feel what your going through, and I 'see' things that may harm you......
for you - you have those gifts too, yet it still amazes me how you're able to see what I 'think' in its clarity and in its truth..."

~ ~ ~

DEFINING MOMENT

"Every moment that we live is a 'defining' moment in time, each step is just as important as the next, all part of the 'life design' ......all determining where the next stop will be, in both our futures to complete you and complete me......that's why each step should be

weighed for the greater good and even if its an unpopular choice, well at least we know we did it after considerable thought......every story has two sides and we have free will to believe, in strife when you feel you have to choose sides before putting stock in what you've been told, best to hear the voices of all parties of which the event unfold.......life and people can be manipulated its true, make you see things that just aren't for you..... like yes its a fact that you fell and lost your way, but the truth is you fell on purpose to use as a weapon on someone you wanted to slay.....ever moment that we live is a 'defining' moment in time like the day you decided I was yours and you were mine......everything that happen after that point was used in a way that lead up to this very day, a day dreamt of so long ago, a beautiful love story once foretold..."

~ ~ ~

P.S. I LOVE YOU

"Sometimes the use of the words are easy for some, "I love you," for others is hard 'til its won......then others say I love you in so many other ways, they keep speaking this language until one day a love so true understands every word and looks straight in the eyes at you......finally you think here is someone who speaks my language and knows me

enough to know my unspoken, I love you, is real and true ......I'm the, I love you, in spoken word type so there is no guessing, and I show you too just to seal the message ......but still I understand when words aren't enough or can't come out for any reason as easy as some, that actions can speak louder than words and in some cases the 'actions' are really lots of fun......but when a person who seldom speaks the words finally says 'I love you' it solidifies the message and seals it like glue..."

~ ~ ~

TOOLS OF FOOLS

"Imagine what MLKJr was going through, in a world filled with distaste for his race and all he knows is God wouldn't want him to hate......meeting attacks with love, healing his pain with song......knowing through a dream that his life wouldn't last long......with that in mind any other man with give up, combat hate with hate and meet attacks with the power of his prestigious popularity and weight......but he did what his Lord would want

him to do, love his enemies and pray for them too......even the militant Malcolm X came back from Mecca with change, enlighten with the fact that hate only continues the pain......that the only thing that can stop hate in its tracks when hate wont, is Love and understanding which gives birth to hope - with hope you'll never break - therefore no victory for hate......and even though he knew picking up the cross of peace would mean he might die, he did it anyway, he did what his Lord would want him to do, love his enemies and pray for them too......I always believed that with the power of Love it opens the doors to a train of thought where solutions can easily walk through...... I believe that there is always a way to combat hate with a simple tool, one that stops it in its tracks makes the hater look like fool......we just need to fix our minds on stopping the problem, not by reprimand, but by takin' away the power of haters tools make them all useless, the tools of fools..."

~ ~ ~

CREATIVE FLOW

"The booster to a geniuses' creative flow is the freedom of letting it show..... but in life if its not your career life suppresses the creative juice, no time to let it

loose.....life says there are other priorities that should take its place, so you pack creativity up, simply pack it away......but every now and then in life it comes out to play, used in life to help you on your way.......I found that to be true for me cause once the opportunity came and I found it odd that my poems ended up in greeting cards......another moment in time I was asked to draw a radio stations' logo, I did and it became a milestone in its history - a story to be forever told......they say creativity is a gift from God and that's a fact I know for sure, its a gift to carry you through life's problems to help you hold on and endure.....that's just one example of how love is, what some cant see, why we're willing to give up self and become one - to become We....its created from God that creative flow, something you know will always be there -helping you grow..."

~ ~ ~

AN ORIGINAL

"So glad that I am a leader set my own trends, I am an original - for to take someone else's characteristics, life experiences and call them my own is so primal......glad that I am a peacemaker, known as the calm during a stormy sea, for to be known as the giver of conflict, hater and one who takes because of greed - its just not me......glad I value the little things in life, like a smile, the beauty of the butterfly,

the dawning of another day, the blessed feeling when seeing a child play...... for to value only ill gain, bank account amounts, materialistic gain - is just not, its just not my way...... because I want it to be said when this life has past, that 'EM' tried to spread love each until the last..."

~ ~ ~

STOP HATING

"The enemy, who I call evil, can only get at you through the use of someone, like the enemies of the world causing destruction by the tons......you take away the portal, you take away his things, then what ever evil throws at you its just not touching......its like someone drunk on control, you just take away the keys and give them a ride to reality - have them walk it off until they see......so when I retreat - when I believe God is not there or when I believe I'm being treated unfair - its to cover up the portals in a way, and it allows me to come back with God to fight my battle another day......its not quitting when you retreat from attacks, sometimes its a strategy to ensure your focus is on having someone's back...... sometimes retreat is

allowing someone to have their way even though you disagree and could have so many negative things you'd want to say......its like a football game, make a defense by getting ahead of the attack game, so no matter what they throw - they wont hit their goal......concentrate on defense not being intense so you're causing strife, with defense when the attacks come - doesn't matter you still high on life......my strategy is to always keep God's love in mind, so I pick my battles and try always to be kind......sometimes with the attacks in life every now and then I need to step away to prevent a fight, like in sports when they stop the game and call a 'time out'...... but as you see and its proven to be true, I'm not caught up in the hate of evil, cause I'm too busy loving you..."

~ ~ ~

MIRACLES HAPPEN

"Miracles happen every day on so many levels and in so many ways......I try to see the miracles in everything, for to see them oh what happiness it brings...hold on to your memories of miracles they're needed, when life gets you down when you're feeling defeated......the memories of the wondrous miracles will bring a warm light seen from miles, just remembering the gift will turn any frown into a smile..."

THE ARTIST IN YOU

"If what I think is happening how cool it will be, to be able to live a life me spoiling you and you spoiling me...people won't understand except those who love the same - the kind of love we share, they will think it strange...... that the depth of our love brings admiration and understanding, that the love evolves - but is never changing......with you I can see how my music will be, it will grow to something that will amaze - even me...... I believe this to be true, because I can tell you love the artist within me too..."

~ ~ ~

TWO BABIES

"One thing in life God wants us to do...be fruitful and multiply - that I leave up to you......He could have arranged your babe's birth this way cause he knew the challenges I would face...... maybe there were things He had to make right, or you just needed time to get things in your life tight......I learned I was right to have patience with haters, I learned the depth of your love for me, that it ran deeper than any sea and higher than any star in the Heavens we can imagine they'd be......maybe we both had to learn without a doubt this love is real, so He gave us time and the gift to "feel".....I saw two babies that day that I woke - of that I am sure, maybe the second one is ours, a gift for what we had to endure..."

~ ~ ~

GREATEST STORY EVER TOLD

"What a story it will be written told in books played out on theater stages, and all kinds of films and difference places......the birth of a love so powerful it transcended all things, looked upon as more valuable than the precious of gems.

......its energy attracting all to come and see - some marvel, some are inspired and others envy......a love that started as innocent as can be, from a time when one day you came to help me.......from that day to this nothing in you I could see wrong, my support of you is still framed on my bookshelf - a remembrance of that help......who would have thought that one day we'd meet in a way where we both had time and the opportunity to see, that the person before us look just like 'me'......the story will say that if there was an Adam and Eve that surely we represent how it must have been when human life first began..."

LOVE LIVES IN THE HEART

"How can one be lonely when someone lives in your heart, longs for your company wishes you were never apart......how can one be a failure when someone loves everything you do, cheers you from the side-  lines, finds pride in every piece of you......how can one feel happy successful when loves not there, when their heart and mind is with someone not there to share.......how can you not be happy when friends are willing to go to the ends of the earth, to make sure you're happy rather than lonely and hurt......how can one be lonely when they have the love of someone so dear a love forever true, how can you have that kind of love and still be blue......How can one be lonely when someone lives in your heart, no more loneliness, no more moods of blue, no more days apart cause that love is always with you soaked through every essence of what makes you, you..."

TO TASTE YOUR LIPS

"The taste of your lips is just as I thought it would be, even the smell of your body when I wake up - you connect to me......the feel of your hands cupping the mounts of my cheeks, the movement of my hands loving the touch of your body next to me...... the warmth of your hug after as we drift off to sleep, is what I feel and taste when its time for our love-flow to go deep..."

~ ~ ~

SAW YOUR FACE

"I see your face every mole, ever scare, the shape of your nose and the lips that make you who you are......I see your messages in your pictures, hear our lives in your songs - my Tiger with eyes of blue, I see you seeing me as clearly as I see you..."

~ ~ ~

CAN'T DEFINE LOVE

"No one can define your love for someone you know, for the meaning in words can never really be told......no one can explain why to you someone is beautiful especially if their older, for beauty is seen only in the eyes of that one beholder......all you can do is show your feelings in actions through time, to show my heart is yours and yours is mine......then one by one they will learn what you been saying all along, that you can't explain it, but in her is where I belong..."

~ ~ ~

THE BUSINESS SHOP

"If I had the power to do whatever I wanted, the first thing I'd do is launch a Fast-Business Shop, open entrepreneurship's door......don't take much I found in all my years, to pinpoint a person's God given talent the reason they were placed here......the talent that makes them a commodity that's hot, the one that makes people say, you're among the best you're at the top.......I'd invest in the building of their dreams without strings,

they own 100% everything......I'd train others to do the same so in the end America will be ahead of the game......when every household can truly say, they will make it either way......more businesses, no 'glass ceiling' jobs, living the American dream won't be so hard......to know in this country your dreams are guaranteed to come true, all you have to do is cash in on your talents and they'd be a million waiting for you......and as America grows from the rise in entrepreneurs, talented workers and scholars to guide, the day of holding one down, begging for unemployment funds will be a thing of the past - we'd have the ideal job the kind that always last...... and for those unwilling to invest in the future and a better day, they will find that moving train will force them to just get out the way......if I had the power to do whatever I want never will a child feel hunger, all medical needs met, have an abundance of love and no more homelessness.......American spirits will be on top, and it will be all due to the 'Fast-Business Shop'..."

~ ~ ~

PEACE

"Peace comes when your heart is on God's journey for you, turmoil comes when you're going in the opposite path,

the one that wont last......peace comes when your words are from a place of love, turmoil comes when your words are not agreeable to The Man above......peace comes when your love is true, turmoil comes when your love only benefits one of you......peace brings a smile to your face even when attacked by hate, turmoil comes when you have no love to give when all you know is take, take, take......between us two the world will find, that peace will always exist between you and I..."

~ ~ ~

DEEP AS THE SEA

"Take the test and you will see, that my love is deep and true as can be......no need to brag about how I treat my man, but lets just say he wouldn't want to be in anyone else's 'hands......take a test and you will see, that your trust can be placed solely in me...... my lips are too loose to hold on to a lie, with the truth there is no need to question why......take a test and you will see, that loving me will be Heavenly..... take this clean slate and mold it to how you want love to be - a symbol of us and how we flow deep as the sea..."

~ ~ ~

SHY LOVE

"Its always those with the biggest shine that wants to shy away...... the ones with the biggest hearts that cry from things that take our breath away......its always the ones with the biggest purse that feels the need to take, take, take......and its the ones with the biggest smile who gets all the hate......but in the end it all evens out - the light will shine for that's its way, the heart will live and find a way, the purse will open no matter what they say, and the glow from the smile with attract love the very next day..."

~ ~ ~

BACK TO EGYPT

"Try taking the sun out of sunlight and you'll have to call it night......try taking the sweet nectar out of flowers and with bees you'll have a fight......try taking sound away from the waves at sea, and life would just be a boring mystery,....,,try taking the Egyptian era out of history, its like saying you're not missing me......cant be done that era is a fact in every way, and so is how you show me you miss me each and every day..."

ROMANCE

"Relationships start with a hello, a backwards glance, a thought on a possible romance - should I take the chance......the hello grows into a need to know more, that blossoms into someone you think you could possibly adore......so the hello turns into a conversation - however it may be - highlighting each others past and hopes for the future, revealing our hidden dreams......that revelation pinpoints the common personality traits, that sparks the day this relationship you had to weigh......how important has it turned out to be, can I live without him - can he live without me......then you realize from that simple hello the door to an eternity of being alone has just been closed, and you realize you need not look for romance any more..."

~ ~ ~

WAKE UP TO YOU

"What a delightful way to wake up with the smell of you and the feel of your touch, those intimate moments just between the two of us...... for a man like yourself those moments are weighed, to get one from you is how I get paid...... you and me meld together as one heart, beating the same rhythm whether to-

gether or apart......what a delightful way to wake up knowing you have a place in someone who love's life, that the memory of you will always be one of delight..."

~ ~ ~

DESTINY

"How could it be that you should meet me, strangers practically, meeting again and again as if by design - I was meant to be yours and you meant to be mine......as the days and months past the dots continue to be connected, we find the reason we were sometimes in life neglected......it was because no one could fill that hole, one Tailor-made to be filled by each others' Souls......we could be in a crowded room, and somehow our focus would to each other zoom.....in another time, another era, another life, the pull would still be constant always gravitating to each others light..."

~ ~ ~

SURE 'NUFF LOVE

"To have a sure love, know you are part of the heart of someone so true to love......a romantic love, that hold your hand love, that kiss you in public love - its truly a blessing......that stand by your side love, no matter what happens ......to have a magical love, that comes with an energy-streams to feed you love, the kind that allows you to always be there when they need you love...is sure 'nuff' the prime-reason Love..."

~ ~ ~

LOVE IS THE KEY

"Love is the reason I do what I do, good or bad choices the goal is to set love free, for those that know me, love sweet love is always been key......it was love that brought me here, to a place I've always held dear...... then it was love that had me

take that call for help, that led me to feelin' your most inner thoughts, a reflection of myself......it was love that's been pushing every decision made since that day, when your love took control......we started to court, like a job interview we talked, until we melted into one, we started beating as one ...... it was love, sweet love that made that bond with me, cause love sweet love is always the only key...... but before we could date suddenly you were gone, but it was love, sweet love that holds me stead so we can move on..."

~ ~ ~
THE BEAST

"I still feel the same pull coming from your direction, hasn't let up only increased in perception......the beast within you is still calling my name, I feel you coming, feel the heat from your flame......with such power there is not much I could do, but surrender to Love and trust my heart to you...."

~ ~ ~
FOREVER HEAR IT

"I said it before, I will say it again, you - I'd follow you anywhere......I'd do this because of your love for me, not only does it protects, it lets me be me......a love like yours breaks the chains that love can bring, hope mine is the same gives freedom so you're always able to sing......for in your voice is the power to move hearts, the depth of your Soul brought to the surface - showing the audience that beautiful Spirit, ensuring them that they will forever hear it...."

~ ~ ~
COMING FOR ME

"Some times if you keep still and focus in on nature, the sounds you hear will give you patience......the songs of the birds as they start their day......the wind dancing with the trees and beautiful butterflies as the move away.......cats in the distance trying to be quiet and petite, while dog barks are the back drop on all you can see......bees as they suckle the honey so sweet, and spiders and ants busy working to build before they sleep.......some times when I keep still and focus on his dream I hear the footsteps of you coming for me..."

~ ~ ~
ONLY YOU

"If they lined up all the eligible bachelors in the world, the most handsomest men with money to do anything for a pretty girl...... men that could physically climb and beat down any wall, nice and built standing

actually ten feet tall......men that could take me around the world, place treasures at my feet, give me pleasures unheard. make my life seem complete.......I'd say I would have to pass even if my living gets harder, money become scarce between both of us two, Id still rather walk the rest of my life with you - only you..."

~ ~ ~

LOVE TRAVELS THE WORLD

"To travel the world what a pain yet a thrill, the pain of confinement and the thrill of seeing what's in pictures too beautiful to be real......places like that are medicine taken through the eyes, the sight travels down to your Soul gives you a feeling you just can't describe......that's a description of our love the feeling it gives is like medicine working from within, keeps you high and its stronger than any wonder man has ever seen......it's what keeps me loving you and you loving me, it's the kind of medicine that leaves you never, like a beautiful diamond it will last forever..."

~ ~ ~

HAVE NO DOUBTS

"How can you give up on a love so true, that which try to separate that love with a wedge is a fool......only good things come from adoration so deep, its the fuel that puts that fire under our feet.....its the support when storms threaten to destroy our house, its the rainbow that tells you never fear, have no doubts..."

~ ~ ~

LOVE IS A SEED

"Seeds can be an idea that grows when you don't even know, grows until the idea becomes a train of thought, a thought that has roots right down to the Soul......where passion lives turning the idea into gold, the golden idea now starts to take form pushing the mind to create a strategy to get the dream going......the body understands what the mind is saying and takes action, and before you can count to ten the strategy is being implemented for the mind and body are one......and as long as that passion burns in the heart of gold, there is no doubt the idea will reach its goal...."

THINKING OF YOU

"You get pulled from the right and the left but I guess, its fun when those pulling you want only the best...... but once the games are over and its time for bed when you're all alone, hope you think of me longing for you to bring me home..."

~ ~ ~

LOVE THE WAY YOU LOVE ME

"Love the way you love me, so supreme so fine, I knew you'd be that special guy, loving and always looking oh so fly......so fly in style, in creativity, your artistry enticed me......I was blinded by your image I couldn't see that you first loved the essence of who I be......the way you loved me, stop me right in my tracks, first thing I saw was how you wore your caps......the way you love me allowed me to take another look, there in your eyes I read you, read you like a book......that's why I knew somehow you'd make a way, no matter how long or what road you had to take I knew there would be this day......I knew I wouldn't walk alone, thanks to your friends that led me to you, they led me home..."

Journey To Love: A Book of Poems
By Eunice Moseley, MS, M.B.A.

Chapter 3

Under Fire

Shortly after he told me his nickname was Bear a video was posted on my Facebook timeline of a Jamie Foxx music video for "Blame it on the Alcohol." It was a clip of a party scene with a man in a bear costume with two ladies on each arm. Either I questioned him about or maybe he knew I was watching it because I saw a post right after that said, "I been out here for a while." Everyone wonders where he has been, but he has been behind the scenes - incognito - hanging with and working producing, and ghost writing for his celebrity friends.

It seems there is a major campaign to keep me and Love apart, and when I say major I mean worldwide, multi-million dollar budget major. He is still talking to me via his friends profiles that I follow. His celebrity friends are now being targeted too.

Well it seems this campaigns' only goal is to get me to stop sending him emails, and to stop me from sharing his picture and content on my social pages. If I do my accounts are hacked and posts deleted. I just repost, and repost.

For not adhering the attacks have escalated to off-line. My family members are now targeted and threatened. My mother and sister have an unusually high number of system manipulation occurrences. My mother started to get anonymous calls from a girl saying that something was wrong with her computer, and lots of hang up calls as well. While helping my mother with her computer problems, the changes to it had to have been by someone with remote access.

Just for evidence of hacking I had my computer scanned, and almost 900 suspicious spyware items were found. They said a normal amount is about 80. My brother found a died cat, cut in half, on his lawn. I am a Leo the lion, a cat, born in August 16th. I took it has a death threat. I did not, and still don't, worry because of my deep Spirituality - it is like a blanket that keeps me calm. I am ex-military, a veteran, and I literally almost died while in service so not much scares me. I was robbed at gun point once, I did not fear death then because my Christian belief tells me absent from the world present with God.

All the things Satan does to get us to turn away from God (and love), and turn to fear (and hate) are being done. Whomever it is, and I am assuming they are Love's former dates fueled by millions or access I believe came from Oprah. The money being spent, the favors being called it, the lengths to separate us as friends is nothing short of evil. How they are controlling them is nothing but legalized slavery. I post on my social a message, "get behind me Satan."

I have no doubt Oprah is involved I am just not sure how or why. I see pictures of Oprah wearing clothes very close to what I wear. She wore a black blouse almost exactly like the one I have . She was on a late night talk show singing a musical song I had recently sung in my home, making reference to something I said in my email to Love.

On the cover of an issue of her magazine she was posed in a position I sleep in. Awkward modeling position I thought - with my hand behind my back. I have chronic joint pains and holding my lower as I sleep helps. Could be why Love is in pictures with his hand behind him. back, knees, wrist, shoulders and neck).

So you may find me with my hand behind my back sitting down as well. I believe Oprah is watching me without my consent.

They openly, in posts, admit to everything. They claim they can't be caught. I call them and their actions evil. Surprisingly they do not deny it, but chastise me for daring to say it.

They brag "I'm stealing your life," because their campaign is to make it seem publicly that he is with someone other than me. They have gone after my clients/contacts via stolen information from hacking my accounts, I believe just to threaten me to back off.

Since they have control over his public image, public content, performance schedule and have the money to get in on projects that he uses to send me messages they have painted a believable public persona that is not true. That's what they mean they stole my life. I post on my social pages "take someone else's life, this one is taken." This is why I publish this book.

One post said that "he won't leave me if I

threaten suicide," of course I told him but from his post I could tell he knew the threat was not real. A subtweet post said "I want my luggage back," referring, I believe, to Love (as property), or maybe the David E. Talbert project film Baggage Claim. One of the projects I could tell they were involved it.

> **(July 11, 2012) Me to Love:**
> "So proud of you guys...so much growth...heard you say 'Beauty I see you.'...my baby Kelly posted a picture of a sign 'ic*E*' with the E red (my favorite color), like I C U (*E*un*ICE*)...all love..."

There are subtweet threats on my life, one said, "either you dying or I am." I welcome every hate filled message because in it is confirmation that my relationship with Love is real - unwelcomed by those hating - but real.

He tells me to keep my principles, to be strong, that he has my back, and to believe in his feelings for me. He sends me messages of love everyday in so many ways. That I start to end my emails with "I see you" so he knows I see them.

Once in a video of his performance he said it back, "I see you."

Not long after my email to him about the use of ICE on social media via his friends profiles, which happens to be letters in my name Eun*ICE*, Kelly Rowland releases a single titled "Ice."

These shout outs are happening with his friends in songs, music videos, movies, commercials, advertisements. The high-profile actors, comedians, singers and even politicians are speaking for him to me. The more love they give the more hate the "attackers" give back. I guess when you make a deal with the devil one day he is going to come and collect.

I tell Love, if the deal was him getting full custody of his son, I'd wait 10 years. In fact, I received a message from God just before Christmas in 2013 that included the number 10 and it came in a way that I took it to mean "new life" - it renewed my hope that it will all work out.

I saw a subtweet threatening his son. I questioned him about that. I said if I didn't know better someone just threaten your son. Shortly after that there was a mass shooting at an elementary school. Then kids in Africa was kidnapped while in school during another threat that I felt was against my grandson. Unbelievable right? But you have to know me to believe I am a very honest and intelligent individual. If you believe me I am sure you will start to see the subtweet conversations and subliminal messages too.

In one year I had two car accidents, been driving accident free for 40 years, my sister had a near accident on November 16th - we both were born on the 16th.

This is when I decided to call the police to file a complaint so there would be a record of what is happening to me. I called first the computer crimes department, Officer Na Ciah, referred me to State Highway police since there was an attempt murder by car allegation. I talked with Sergeant Marie Manilpella at State Highway and she said she didn't have the staff to investigate, but I got the feeling she did not believe me.

I went back to Officer Na Ciah and he said he would look into it, but he has not returned my follow calls. I then called the local police. I talked to Officer Dillion and Sergeant Felipo (who returned my call to Sergeant Sine - Officer Dillions' supervisor), and he said I needed more evidence. They told me to print the screen of any threats on social media.

I then filed a complaint with the local FBI. I still reach out to the local police with updates of what I consider is evidence. In a follow up conversation with Sergeant Felipo he told me that the FBI are probably working on my case now. In fact, I received a recorded message from the FBI acknowledging receipt of my complaint. This is another reason for publishing *Journey to Love...* - documented evidence.

I started to fear for his life when I realized his former dates that were certainly part of those attacking me were still part of his staff or business. They post about what they would do to him the next event when they see him again. Calling him a sex slave and other claims that had me so worried about him I started to end my emails with "eyes open," "don't sleep," and "Come back to me."

When you are a billionaire or millionaire you have developed influences and connections in high places, just the mention of your name people believe what you say as gospel. Your name makes them have no doubt or question you, because of how much money you have or the things you have gained.

They boldly brag in subtweets posts "I own them", or "I wish they would say something"- meaning Dru Hill and SisQo. But Love speaks to me through his friends.

I don't back away that easy from a challenge. People who know me know this to be true. I am also Spiritually strong in my belief that God has control over all, and that he is a good God. So when I think its something God wants me to do, like support my friend who came to me in need and could be in distress and not able to speak for himself, an offer of a billion dollars would not make me stop.

I start to see subtweet posts and movie scenes and script lines that indicated interest in the companies could have been sold. That post was followed by a post saying that he needed the money to pay debts. I email that I can understand that. Sometimes in order to be free of something you have to sacrifice something else. His message also said that the control had an end date.

While fighting the battles we developed a stronger friendship while trying to balance out the fake public image they are projecting with the truth. I believe because of subtweet posts that even our haters are impressed by our commitment to each other.

Chapter 3 is titled "Under Fire," it is about how our battle turned into a war in Hollywood.

~ ~ ~

NOTHING NEW

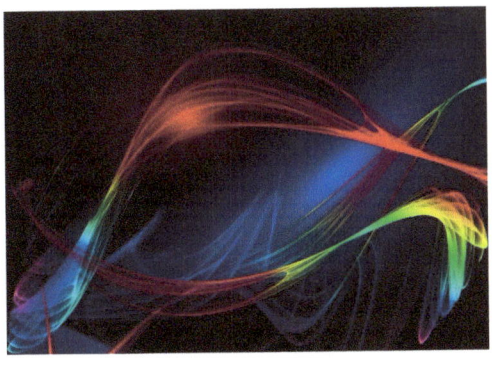

"Nothing's new under the sun, but what's new is this love, love strong enough to make two simple people becoming one......a love with such energy it has one purpose through time, to show the power of love to all mankind..."

~ ~ ~
LOVE MOVES MOUNTAINS

"No matter what the situation that I'm facing, all I have to do is look at you and all cloudy skies become clear and blue......all mountains become small mole hills, suddenly hate thrown at me, I just don't feel......I'm willing to take a step into the unknown just from what I feel, willing to go through any storm face any 'alkalis heel'..."

~ ~ ~
JUST LIKE YOU

"I'm so proud of you, the feeling is beyond what any drug could do, the influence you have on the world, who wouldn't want to be your girl......the whole world stops when you say your search is done, everyone wants to know which beauty will be the one......not only has God given you riches that's coming in waves, but He gave you perfectly made children to love and to raise......what an honor, what a joy to be your child - like you - I have two—whom I love to make smile...... what an honor it would be to raise a baby that's new, with a little face of a boy or girl that looks just like you..."

~ ~ ~

THE END OF TIME

"Another cloudy morning, but I wake up with a smile, thanks to you my thoughts are of sunshine - the warm and loving kind......I already know how you will treat me, cause it has been ordained since the beginning of time that i will spoil you and you me - that you will always be mine......and me, from what I see, I'm a collection of many women you love(d), a complete package designed by the Heavens up above......like all good things in life the risk to have is high, its something though we have to face until the end of time..."

~ ~ ~

ONE-MATE DREAM

"Bet never in your dreams did you imagine this life change, heart so connected you start traveling in the one-mate lane......be in a position to be with that one special one, someone who you adore, that someone who would love you down to the core.....time is of no consequence when God has His hand in it, when you're looking to spend a lifetime with someone, giving up a few months or years is just part of what has to be done.......we're all looking for a lifetime partner, when you look at them you see yourself, know with out a doubt there could never be someone else......bet you never knew it would end-up this way on the same lifetime team, but then again maybe you did, maybe you had your own dream..."

~ ~ ~

READY MADE FAMILY

"Take your time, do what's right, let your heart lead you for it will affect the rest of your life......I'm so at ease, your love gives me peace, there's not much I could ask of you cause you're so sweet......so take your time love, do what's best for your life, believe that I see

you working your way towards me, with an already made God given family..."

~ ~ ~

BET YOU'D LOOSE

"If they bet that I will stop loving you they will loose, bet that we are not one and they'll find themselves looking at me and seeing you......If they bet you are not my world its proof that they refuse to see, they'll find themselves in a world of make believe unable to deal with reality...... If they bet that in time our feelings will change they will loose, they keep following us waiting for the end - but they may just be wearing out their walking shoes......If they bet they can confuse me have me drowning in doubt - a slave to time cant find my way out, they will loose so why should I get upset and at them shout.....If they bet things will change they will loose and that's a fact, cause now that we found love we're never letting go, yes the odds say better to bet on that ..."

~ ~ ~

MY HERO

"It takes a hero to hang on tight, to go through fire, to take a chance to not give up the fight......what makes a hero, is a controversy in itself, but its simple enough to me, its one who simply helps......a hero thinks of his/her fellow-man before him/herself... they help just because they can, they reach back and simply lend a hand, not to some, they don't pick and choose, a hero helps every creature with a Soul, like me and like you…"

~ ~ ~

I LOVE PICTURES

"I love pictures, done right they can be more creative than a painting, more informative than a book ......with just one glance, yes all you need is just one look......so why is it I don't like my self in pictures, can't understand it but its a fact, I love pictures but they don't love me back..."

~ ~ ~

CAN'T GET THROUGH

"Nice to know you are always by my side, never was lonely but having you with me makes me smile......we  are each others' angel sent from the Man above, our only duty - protect and to endlessly love......a love that will make you go through hell take the bullet even if it kills, a love that makes us hold on with all of our will......doubters don't understand cant figure out our plan, but I know Love what you have to do, what you're going through......for this purpose God gave me a talent the ability to understand what others can't see - means none of the BS gets through to  me......so feel safe in knowing I'm with you always and that there's nothing the world can do, nothing people could say to make me think any other way..."

~ ~ ~

LET IT GO

"Can anyone be as proud of you as I, you are the apple - I am sure - of your mothers eye......can anyone love you as much as I do, I - who see God at work every time I look at you......can anyone match you as well as this Soul can, so much as one - its as if we were united at the moment that life began......they say if you love something don't be afraid to let it go, if it's meant to be - in life - it will soon show......I loved you that much that letting go was not a fear, for I had no doubt that your love was real..."

~ ~ ~

FREEDOM

"People take freedoms for granted until they are taken away, then you realize how easy in life it is for others to legally take what freedoms you have - people take it to be sold and think its ok......but I hope my love for you has made you free, as your love has done for me......no matter what happens in the future one thing I know is real, that this love, this magical energy called love, that we both feel ..."

THE SON

"What a gift the Sun is, gives life to flowers, sight for eyes to see, that's what your loving does for me...... its warmth goes deep, deep where it planted a seed, a seed others are just now beginning to see......It grew uniting us as one, way before our lives had begun.....therefore its logical to think by anyone where this love began, its started by the gift we call the Son and The Man..."

~ ~ ~

FREE TO BE

"Love allows you to be free, free to be truthful without fear, free to go and come, cause whether physical or in Spirit love is always there always near......love is selfless, no longer worrying about 'what about me,' loves only goal is to you it wants to please......free to dress in a way that makes you feel fine, knowing love is still proud to 'make you mine'......love believes in you when everyone else says don't, cause love just can't let you walk that road alone......so then who I often wonder would choose money over love, something you just can't buy no matter how hard you try...... cause love is like the air, you cant see it but its life-giving power is always there......to give love away the power would certainly fade, cause the power of love, called 'real love' to separate it from the rest, is tied to one special person who past the 'real love' test........Love its often imitated but never do they come as close to the love that allows you to be free, free to be without walls, able to reach higher than you can imagine and never ever fall ..."

~ ~ ~

YOUR BACKPACK

"Take me with you close by your side, close like your backpack first thing you pick up when you leave, treat me the same keep me polished like your silver chain......know you can put your valuables in me and know they will be there when you get back, never have to fear pain because of me and that's an actual fact......I'll be your help-mate, friend, and lover, make you so happy you won't need another..... for one backpack is all you'll ever need when you put your heart and trust inside of me..."

~ ~ ~

TRUE LOVE

"Saw your message and I feel the same, I understand its hard when your placed in that separation game......separation ain't no joke but one thing aside from destroying a relationship it does, it also is the big tester of whether its true Love.....if in all this time your heart is still with me, what else but true love could this be..."

~ ~ ~

MY ANGEL PROTECTS

"My angel who watches over me, some are so blind with envy they can't see, in your heart is where I will always be......nothing they can say or do that will change that fact, but they will try and try so their lies can be a fact......if you are strong and hold on to love we will be one my best friend, I been here before if your love is true I know how it will end......my angel protects me in everyway, so to the haters I still have nothing to say..."

~ ~ ~

FOREVER SUNSHINE

"It's cloudy outside, but all I see is the sun with the memory of your smile, such a familiar one......the thought of how you speak to me, so romantic in every way, the conversation behind the conversation that's how you play......to be with you and yet not, I don't know about you but that concept is very hot......what a wondrous gift we have hope it forever last, that it always be the sunshine behind the clouds sunshine that will never pass..."

~ ~ ~

YOUR LAKE

"I'd follow you anywhere, Paris, Italy, Santa Fey......two lights together at last, there won't be anything that will matter that comes at us from the past......our eyes are on the future where our dreams wait, a place where there is only "I" in your lake..."

~ ~ ~

THERE IN YOUR PAST

"It's hard to explain waiting a life time for a thing that can last, finding it and discovering it was already there in your past......unfortunately you wasn't looking up at the time, and it went on its way searching for that forever kind......you wondered why didn't the bell ring, why didn't you see, why now did you find that love that makes you totally complete......that something that not many get to feel in a life time, but God supplies you, you just have to watch the signs...... so in life keep your head up don't let it pass you by, I've been bless to experience it twice - that love, that forever survives.....that Love that makes everything ok, something you'd lay your life down for, cause you know 'this Love' God gave - it will endure...."

~ ~ ~

NEVER LONELY

"How can I be lonely when you live, now that I found you and the love you give...before it was my own personality that kept me entertained, but today its you I can feel I'm always there somewhere in your brain......fitting me in your life has always been your goal, to include someone, you feel, is that one perfect girl......one with a heart so gentle and sweet, but yet strong enough to withstand rumors, hate and defeat, one who knows that Love is the key......me needing someone with a true faith in God, and not in ones self, one that knows with Me and You, we don't need anyone else......its the True Love we share that will make our greatest dreams come true, that's what 'they' fear that we'll reach the moon, that our wonderful dream will overshadow their prediction of doom..."

~ ~ ~

LOVE SO PURE

"I love white but it doesn't agree with my red lips, but white is one of my favorite colors I wish I could wear it ...... white so angelic and pure, unblemished by stain, a symbol of Heavenly love so pure, an unbreakable chain..."

~ ~ ~

TALK TO THE ANIMALS

"I love to talk to the animals since as long as I can remember and they always talked back, a connection that can't be explained they understand me and I understand them - and that's a fact......I think they are so very cleaver the best friend of man, people think they are not intelligent with no feelings or souls, but every creature under the sun has a story to be told......without talking they sense your feelings they know instinctively what you want to say, they give love consistently in every single way......like children they depend on us to care and brighten up their days, for we are the center of their being, when we look at them its our humanity that we are seeing...... they want us to share what we have all they want is for us to truly care, care enough to love them back and its been proven an animal can lengthen your life - and that's a fact......so I talk to the animals big and small, the medicine that eases my strife, animals are the highlight of my life..."

~ ~ ~

100 THINGS AT ONCE

"I saw in your eyes your mind working on 100 things at once, I was so in tune to you
I could probably name every last one.......but what amazed me most, you wasn't missing a beat each one you were on top - at the utmost......but remember love, what you have is a gift and to some doing that, they would be mystified, something they wouldn't have the skill to do even if they tried.......the blessing is with such a superior brain, you - my heart - treat everyone exactly the same.........I saw also in your eyes your need to have me near, and with Gods help Love I'm still here.........the day after the expo when I said that prayer to the Master, He said He'd make you whole if I'd support you - even in the life-after.........He kept His promised as I knew He would for me, and it seems I've kept mine, even though life didn't make it easy......I've come to learn the reason being is because Love is the key, so I hope Love you said a prayer for me..."

~ ~ ~

BEAT IN EVERYTHING

"Did you know there's a beat in every-thing under the sun, it's as if God so love music that He made sure it's present in everything He created - everything has the ability to create music so basic.......rain drops, the beat of big and little feet, even ones heart has a beat......no wonder music is a universal language, one that can not be misunderstood, comes at you simply - giving only good......did you know I can use every part of me to make a beat, that's why I've always said I am Music and Music is within me...."

FOR THE BETTER

"I saw you love, and I feel the same, my life too has changed for the better since you came........it's that love

-flow I'm sure it is, feeding me energy helping me push full speed ahead.......if that's true then it's the same for you, my love energy has you on a special high, something no one can understand - that no man can describe.....but I see you Love and it's nice to know when it seems no one can be true, that you are with me - still - in everything I do..."

~ ~ ~

THE PART

"I love feeling you, it speaks to me in a way that makes me smile, I bet its hard to believe you have someone with the same desires, same mind, same heart, that of a loving kind.......I know now I was sent here to protect, He would use me for His love project......as a thank you, God gave me a brave heart, you - the only one who could play the part and be true.."

~ ~ ~

THE PLAY

"I now know I was placed in a play without knowing that I was in the act, I stum-

bled on my part and the audience laughed, some of them even wanted their money back.......the plays heartless producer - for laughter - wanted me to fall, and I did stumble until I saw you in the audience then I gave it my all......I kept my 'eyes on you' sitting in a front row seat, your eyes said simple - just follow my lead..."

~ ~ ~

PRECIOUS JEWEL

"We are both precious jewels to be protected, made with a substance called Love that, like diamonds, will last forever.......we've gone through so much pressure, like diamonds, we can't help but shine, 'til the world can see that I belong to you - and you will forever be mine..."

~ ~ ~

MY NEW HOME

"I went through every step to lay down roots, be a foster parent and then my life changed, it led me on a road here where nothing is mine - nothing is the same.......I had to give up my properties, my job, my life, and I was told, I had to give away all these things to find my new home..."

I SEE HOME

"Its one thing to see a person on screen and in a pictures, its a shadow of the real person & the looks can play tricks......but to see a person in the flesh is the ultimate test, to see if the looks are for show or if the person moves something deep in your chest.......the chest where there is a place called home, where your personality is free to roam.......We live in that place deep within each others' chest, where we're free to be, we can be open for all to see, so I am glad you had another chance to once again - see me..."

~ ~ ~

REFLECT

"I'm taking a minute to reflect today, on all the things to me you've said......and how it is that my response was so profound, that on my behalf you stood your ground.......taking time to reflect on all the messages to me in your Art you've placed, just so I wouldn't forget your loving face......swallowed up by a life not set on me, but how you've went to the ends of the world to make sure we'd meet..."

LOVE RULES

"So glad love rules my life, every action contemplating lessening strife as I pray, hoping those who live a different way - full with negative hearsay - can see me as an example of how to live, even when what comes at you is negative.......my life is full of positive uplifting tones, I use them to write my own life's song.......those songs run in my head, until life to me is fed....... then I let the songs take me to another place, a place where hope and love has a new face.......a face that's' kind and patient, the image of me, a face that controls all energy like no other, for the face is love the forgiving Mother..."

~ ~ ~

LOVES' PASSION

"Passion makes you do things, makes you say things sometimes not who you are, the pressure cooker always making dishes, always preparing the for the passionate love wishers........love is the fire that regulates us both, if you're good at loving me, you will be the first to know........if its real

you'll have peace, pressure disappears and doubt falls from your shoulders to your feet...... only thing lift is loves' heat, the heat that makes you do things, makes you say things you really do mean, the pressure cooker making dishes for the passionate love wishers..."

~ ~ ~

WARRIOR FOR LOVE

"Love laughing its such a thrill makes you high off of the real......love music any form or shape, cause its a glimpse into a person's inner space.......love to love cause it brings a certain romance to life, hate negativity brings so much unnecessary strife.......always a warrior for love, will go to war until God says its enough......a protector of the peace that love makes, that's what you will find in my inner space..."

~ ~ ~

WHO'S MONEY

"We have to be careful when suggesting that God is the reason for our riches and major successes, equating that as confirmation of living according to His Word, properly learning his life les-

sons........because in this life, as told by the Bible, there's a period where Satan will rule, so how do we know it isn't Satan's reward for the things that we do.........Our God is a simple loving God who promises that OUR riches are in Heaven, would He help hold one child down while lifting another just because one is Lucky Number 7?.........we know He will open doors that lead to an abundance for those that live according to His Word, but don't be fooled by where your wealth comes unless you've heard..........for riches from God are proven in ones deeds, does that person use his wealth to help others in need?..."

~ ~ ~

LET'S TAKE A JOURNEY

"Lets take a journey together, one that rules in love, and anyone not abiding will pay the penalty there of - that penalty is Love......they must be bounded with an unbreakable bond, bounded with those that give, give only the Master's love.......His Word will be our covenant though sometimes harsh it will be. but as long as we do it His way our Spirit will forever soar

free.......free to Love, free to smile, free to embrace your fellow man, even the haters standing near by trying to prevent it as hard as they can.......for us there will be no exclusions, though you may be asked to leave shown the door, but our door will be forever open to those with Love - if that's what they are looking for..........lets take a journey I'll show you a way of looking at man-kind that no one has ever seen, you will show me the world in parts that could only be describe as a dream..."

~ ~ ~

RUN AFTER ME

"I don't compete for men, play games or fight over them, they are free to go, I carry no chains to bind him........who wants to be with someone not sure  where they want to be, who fights over a man that doesn't - your love - see.......love only last when its a sure thing, when I give my love it always assured he will always be free....... my love can always see and appreciate the good that's all I see, never will I run after a man - he'd be running after me......I don't compete for men, play games or fight over them, I follow a sure love where ever he leads, but you find that he is the one running after me..."

CHILDREN

"Children they didn't ask to come here, so its our responsibility to make sure their stay is as pleasant as possible - one lived with no fear.......that when we leave this world they are secure in life and is active in Spiritual growth - can live through any fight......they are empty vessels needing us to fill, protect them from harm and give them that loving will......help them form that personality that's set at 7, so when we die we are secure that they will reach God's Heaven..."

~ ~ ~

LOVE'S RIDE

"Life takes us for a ride we seem to have no say in the drivers direction, we can only slow it down or speed it up and along the way learn life's lessons........you slowed your ride down to give me a lift, as you were riding along life's highways I gave you some life tips.......but before you could use them the driver said I don't like what she said, they dropped me off blocked the roads so I couldn't get ahead.........the driver felt my tips would lead you to become a reckoning force, so I was left by the wayside as life continued on its

course.....along the way you used my tips learned how to get further, you went from a passenger to the designated driver ....the road went from dirt to paved fit for the Furious Fast 7, one that no doubt makes you think its a road to paradise - next stop Heaven.......but just before you got to those pearly gates you thought of me and turned around in hast.....you told the gate-keeper there is someone we left who helped me get to this place, I have to go back I have see her face........ something no one had ever done, give up paradise to go back to where it all begun, and when you arrived I was still waiting there warmed by the light of the Son.......I was still trying to think of a plan, one that would pave my way to see you again....... I had hoped that you would take me with you to that special land, then I looked up and saw you reaching out your hand..."

~ ~ ~

LIVE FOR FAMILY

"Family life its what we're here for, to leave your parents home and start your own core.......to have someone always to you be fair, always being able to depend on them to care....... knowing you can turn your back, cause they'd always be there - no maybes but a fact......family comes in all forms, but its the extended family

that is the core....... that core that moves with you as life goes by, they're the living example of who you are their main focus is to lift you higher........so most take their time in choosing that 'core', knowing for Love is the only reason you'd create one for.......family life is what we're here for, to leave our footprints on life in the people that we adore..."

~ ~ ~

WE'RE LIKE GHOST

"Down to earth that's what I love about you, you live like you don't know your worth, but yet you've been God's favorite since birth.......He's made my life special too I find, I think I'm one of the apples of His eye........the more you show me your life, the part that impresses me most, is that you live life as a ghost......as you can see, that's how I like to be... undercover no parts of my life showing, I come and go without anyone knowing.......it don't take much to please me, don't need fancy clothes, cars, or diamond rings so all can see...... my wealth is how you make us we, I will now always feel complete in your love for me...."

HOLDING ON

"Its one thing to have someone who wants you cause of the things you bring to their life, but its another to have someone who needs you because you are their light........one kind wants to take and hide you and never let go, and the other needs to give you space so that your light can grow.......we want and need each other it seems, we hold on until our hands bleed ..."

~ ~ ~

GOD'S FAVORITE

"I'm taken away by your passion, its the glue that keeps your group going, Jazz is the versatile voice the power that keeps the group flowing, the suaveness of Nok, the Rock-N-Roll star, is what keeps the group together, and Tao the tenor is what keeps the groups' vocals in Heaven... I'm so impressed with how your guys keep it to-

gether........individually you all are stars no doubt, but together you create an explosive blinding light …....a light that will never die, cause God told me you're the Peach of His eye..."

~ ~ ~

MY BACK

"It's nice to know that in this world there is one to have your back, that someone you can depend on to always know where you're at........it's hard to find that in a world full of imperfect beings, but one thing we can depend on is the love we too are seeing......a love that will never alter who we are inside, only build us up to higher heights as here's why....... this love is the kind that forever grows and unfolds, where time, people, situations, mountains and storms can't stop it from hitting its mark, because our love is the light in a world that's dark.......it's the smile when we need to be lifted, the beat when we need people to listen....... its the sweet loving words we hear constantly in our ears, encouraging us whispering, 'its ok I'm here'.......it's nice to know that in this world there is one to have your back, that someone you can depend on to always know where you are at..."

~ ~ ~

LOVE YOUR MUSIC...

"Love your music how you put together a song is so profound, what a gift to have - I've fallen in love with your art of sound.......I can tell your music because its all about love, it tells a deep story its fresh not similar to anything that was........the lyrics are of triumph, and lots of party fun, no evil intent, no revenge or talk of hurting anyone........it's all about the light good times and showing me you care, even your films are uplifting woven with our romance - you have us everywhere.......love your music, its what I call myself when people are curious as to who I may be, I say my name is Music, cause I am music and music is within me..."

~ ~ ~

Journey To Love: A Book of Poems
By Eunice Moseley, MS, M.B.A.

Chapter 4

Full Armor

The campaign to separate Love and I includes a scripted reality show, where they are trying to make it seem - to the public and me - that he has married (at least three times it has been implied). His post are no I am still a single dad.

His reality show with his son that he posted about, was to be called "SisQo and Kid." He posted about it on is Instagram account before it was deleted.

Then I see post about him starring in a reality show called "Wife Swap." From what I can see it seems to be spliced together - maybe his reality show with someone else's. When I saw it I stopped emailing him. Figured I was played, but I was still watching their recent performances praying they continue to look happy.

I saw a performance of them singing their song "I Love You." Love was singing and he turned around to face the drums and lead guitar, and animatedly pointed down to the floor with his right hand as if he was saying "stay here." Then he turned around and sang the word "stay" so emotionally I cried. I emailed asking if that was a message to me. He posted that all is not what it seems.

The drums he turned to are a symbol of me because I am always drumming on surfaces, even my body. If you know me you know I am a human beat-box. The lead guitar he turned to, well he knows I use to own a red one that I played from high school to my mid-20s.

When I told him at the beginning of the relationship that I was shy, an introvert, with a phobia about pictures he posted a picture of him in a T-shirt with a girl turned backwards, her hair to the side like mine was at the E3 expo and she as naked. See he knows, since he is virtually here with me, that I sleep naked.

So when he was animatedly indicating to the drums and guitar to stay. I knew he meant me.

Shortly after Rihanna released a single titled "Stay." She is in a bath tub. I emailed to Love how I haven't had a bath, only showers, since moving to California. In her "Diamonds" single video she is also floating in a lake. I told Love to date me I have to be the only one in his lake, even wrote a poem about it. Also I told him of my experience in the Navy boot camp I could not swim but they had me float for 5 minutes to past the class. Rihanna in Diamonds (the last name of his ghost account) is floating in what appears to be a lake.

Chris Brown like Rihanna has our story in his songs. In a picture he has a red scarf around his right knee with the fu*k-you finger sign. I sleep in a red scarf, the worst joint pain comes from my right knee, and I told him some at the newspaper I work for call me "U" - U (short for my name Eunice - the E is silent).

> **(October 13, 2012) Me to Love:**
> "My baby Chris Brown was painting a Muriel (around his red pool)...a Muriel btw that has a RED lady with WHITE hair with big boobs lol…"

Around this time most his celebrity friends were wearing a white streak in their hair, like me. I was born with premature grey streak in my hair. Always had a long string of it in the front. Last ten years its crowning the front of my hair s as well. When Love or his friends take a picture with their wool caps, hats and scarves pulled about an inch or so back I know it's a shout out to me cause that's where my grey hairs, aside from the streak, around my temples.

I also LOVE the color red and I was seeing them dressed in a lot of red. I actually dress in all black since my late husbands death, and all black is a symbol for me as well.

I started to email him again cause he wanted me to stay - if you believe. He indicated that the reality show was not what it is being portrayed. I already know to the extent they will go, so I believed him.

As I looked closer at the promo-picture for the show I could tell that the photo of him, which is his son and adult daughter, was photo shopped and merged with a picture of his supposed "wife." In 2014 his supposed "wife" publicly labels herself his girlfriend - to me that confirms what he said that him being married as they tried to indicate many times is not true.

I remembered reading posts of a conversa

tion from someone to Oprah's twitter account. They asked her if she wanted to see the finished cut (indicating a film). That they were finish putting it together. I remember thinking at the time they were talking about a reality show.

Via my lawyer, his friend and baby sitter, and his celebrity friends posts the story he tells me is totally different from what is being portrayed publicly.

The lengths that they are going to - such as the death threats; attempted murder by car; scripted reality aka arranged situations; stalking me; hacking my system and virtually invading my privacy to gain information to target my clients and contacts to threaten my livelihood; going after my car (it was repossess and loan company could not explain why my arrangements made was not ad hid to); intercepting my mail (postal and emails), and anything computerized connected to me they access just so I know thy are stalking me still.

I decided to publish my emailed poems to Love in order to document the true story of what happen to him, that all is not what it seems, and to document what is happening to me.

We are still under heavy attacks. He is using his media interviews, promo videos, celebrity friends films and scripts, print advertisements, digital and broadcast commercials, television shows, music videos, promotional picture's stances (as is his celebrity friends) to tell the true story - to keep me encouraged.

I read a post I believe was Love or someone in control, as I suspect is Oprah, talking to someone that they gave them 5 years. That would coincide with the "end date" of 2016 I keep seeing—from 2011 to 2016 is 5 years.

I believe it's the same amount of time he has to serve under house-arrest. If the posts and messages are correct he will be "free" in 2016.

So until then they can paint a picture that is not true saying he is anything but what he really is. Someone could murder someone and make it seem as though he did it, and its nothing he can do - publicly. The new drama "How to Commit the Perfect Murder" is no coincidence. As I write this the new "CSI: Cyber" series is no coincidence. The film Black Hat about hackers is no coincidence. The president targeting hackers abroad and at home, is no coincidence.

They are always trying to find a chance to threaten me. I had sent a job application to Morgan State University, where I hold a Bachelors degree in Telecommunications. I called up one of the Deans, who I use to intern with when he owned a television production company, to follow up on my application for a faculty position.

A day later comedian/actor Tracey "Morgan" is hit by a Wal-Mart truck. Through a part-time job, my sister and I, we go to Wal-Mart to service products for clients. For me this also was no coincidence.

I believe these allegations to be true because I am living it. It is supported by what the posts say, the timing of the post and the visuals (i.e., poses, what they are wearing, hair styles, captions) I think there is plenty of evidence.

Whomever is speaking on social media via sub tweeting makes sure its clear enough for all who know of this situation to read . They clearly post "I own them." To them I read "you shouldn't have trusted me," and "you should have read the contract." Confirms there is a "contract" involved. Maybe it's a 5 year contract that will end in 2016.

Is slavery legal via contracts in America just because you forgot to read it? Seems unconstitutional that anyone can sign away their public rights to be, to do, to talk. I know record labels did this in the past which lead to a revolution of independent record labels forming across the country. They would make the artists sign away their names, their right to perform in public, and so much more.

At the suggestion of the local police I have printed out screen shots of some of these posts and sub tweets and forward them as "evidence.".

I returned a call to a New York City Detective Josh, who (supposedly) could not remember why he called me. Right after I hung up from him there was a Twitter post with the words at the end 'good luck", which had nothing to do with the rest of the post.

Since Detective Josh never called back I am assuming he was paid off, a fake detective or influenced in some way to make a call to me so I can see the level of their influence or power. Maybe they thought I would be scared enough to drop my complaints with the authorities. Not long after, maybe a day, a video trailer of a new cartoon of Madea (i.e. Tyler Perry) appeared on my Facebook timeline with Madea saying "I am the police, got to protect the children." Most know that Tyler Perry is Madea, and he and Oprah are in business together.

I remember being at an event and something happen behind me, one of those scripted reality situations, but a guy behind me said sarcastically "if its ok with Oprah," I got the impression that comment was meant for me.

As one police stated, I may need to hire my own detective. But if "they" have millions available, they can just buy off the investigator that I hire. So I decided to stick with the FBI, do my own investigation, and collect and pass on that information/evidence to the authorities, and pray for the best. God do not like ugly, in no one.

I was told, by a local Sergeant Felipo that the FBI takes a long time and to be patient,

This chapter "Full Armor," takes us through some of the battles. Some we won, some we lost. Such as a time when I do believe he felt it was over and he was free to be back on retainer with me, and start "dating" me because someone called to talk my business/PR consult. We made a 5 p.m. appointment to discuss his business needs. As I was talking to him I could tell it was Love, but wasn't sure. He sounded like my friend, but I could tell he was disguising his voice so I didn't let him know I suspected it was him.

Once, while covering an event for my syndicated column, I was at a night club and it was dark. As I went to leave I had to squeeze by a very big guy and a guy about my height. In order to squeeze by I had put my left hand on the guy my heights chest for balance. As I was walking down the street, I suddenly knew the guy my height was Love. I realized when I touched his chest I felt a chain, which he is famous for wearing. I am known for always wearing a chain as well - silver cross chains.

That open door must have closed on him because the "guy" did not call back as he said he would. I asked Love in an email if that was him because they guy sounded like my friend and I know all members of the group talk a like.

During Love's next performance he held his hand up - I took it to mean yes it was me on that 5 p.m. conference call. He told me recently it was a "high-five" for you guest right.

We are still focused on each other. have learned now to totally ignore the scripted reality life they keep trying to put me in. He is focused on keeping my attention filled with the truth of the situation; watching his back and mine; sharing with me in pictures how he is raising his son "alone," and including me in his all of many projects .

~ ~ ~

I know I will see him, as he said, "as soon as that door opens" again.

~ ~ ~

CONNECTING THE DOTS
DECEMBER 28, 2012

"You been with me since day one, that day under the Son……..you attached yourself to me before I knew you were there, and there you stayed even to today...I felt your love for me before I knew what it was, didn't understand it, just knew it was sent from Heaven up above...an answer to a life-long prayer, but it seems I had to be fit, I had a life time of lessons to learn before I could have It...I bet your story is quit the same, always asking where's my beauty - always the 'where is she' game...lost in a sea of dating one in-the-same, then that day under the Son came when He said you are now ready to know her name...what a struggle it must have been, knowing the search was finally over, but suddenly life is not allowing you to hold her...then your desire for me turned every thing around you into fire, turned your passion into blue flame igniting a never before seen contagious fire...The fire even burned away you're blinders, you began to want a life a bit more kinder...first task at hand you had to face, get me to see your 'real' face...it seems it was a face I knew all too well, one my mind wouldn't let me see, afraid I wouldn't be able to handle it my heart was too weak...before my eyes saw the 'real' you, you were just The Dragon not the man I 'always' knew...when I saw you I could do nothing but drop to my knees and ask God for help....I saw within you the answer to my life-long prayer, the only one in the world I knew I could trust to care.... something life took from me many years ago, always knowing in my heart it wasn't suppose to be so...with the loving Spirit of my late playing cupid he took his shot, you saw his picture and connected the dots.....you found your passion for me wasn't crazy or a young man in a crush, you finally won the 'where is beauty' game - you finally know her name..."

MUSIC IS EVERYTHING
APRIL 7, 2013

"You'll find my legs are always moving, bouncing to an unheard beat.......its the music in me, you can't hear it like me........music is always ringing inside my head, people talk and a word can trigger a song, as they talk my mind has gone on...... my mind is imagining me singing those words to them, that's how I think - because music is everything..."

~ ~ ~

MANY CULTURES THAT'S ME
APRIL 6, 2013

"I'm made of many cultures, but I love the Spanish culture their branded red and black is so supreme, I love their use of red lipstick, and the artistic way they roll when they sing.......I love their love of family, hard work and the way they kiss and are built...oh but most of all I love the Asian culture their humbleness and the fabrics they use - like silk.......Love their work ethics, their flair and style, how without blinking they'd walk that extra mile.......I could go on about the cultures I love, but I must mention the Native Indians their so close to my heart....... Love their pride, love of family, their oneness with nature, how their known for loving, never hating.......each culture has something great to give to the world that's close to who I am called, like everything about your culture - I love them all..."

~ ~ ~

MEETING YOU
APRIL 8, 2013

"Meeting you has changed my life for the good, I knew that would be the case, I knew it would help me keep the pace...... the pace for what I knew would come to be, I know everything will work out and everyone will see......in the mean time God's love-energy gift to us has passed the test, that love-energy flow we share that's felt whenever my hand rest on your chest..."

BETWEEN US
APRIL 5, 2013

"When you have friends that are there no matter what you decided to do, whether it turns out to be right or wrong they still stick with you........that kind of love only makes you strong, the love that takes is draining and oh so wrong........people wonder why when you squeeze too tight the person normally leave, its the confinement that makes you want be free......so it's nice to have friends that love you no matter what, that's the kind of love we share between us..."

~ ~ ~

LOVE-FLOW
APRIL 4, 2013

"How do you explain an unseen chain that keeps us connected - makes you say, 'I love her,' its a connection of a substance like no other.......what had God had in mind when He decided that His love would have this device, a device where when

He puts two people together in His Love they never have to think twice.......that with this love no time or space can cut off that love-flow, that real-time live-stream that forever consistently grows..."

WHEN YOU FALL
APRIL 3, 2013

"Pleasing the one you love should be your ultimate goal, when you love someone you want to give them riches untold......unless its joy coming from their eyes, how can you love someone and make them cry....... treat them like a possession, a trophy, a toy, love can't cause love understands your feelings its that which everyone is looking for......like a parent you measure your moves by how they will affect those you love, you look for direction from the Master in Heaven above.......His voice is kind and understanding He gives you His all, He fights for the underdog to make sure they don't fall.......yes love is the same at the end of the day, it is like our Love it will conquer all and protect us from the fall..."

~ ~ ~

SHY
APRIL 1, 2013

"I've always been shy, never questioned why, think its because of that old emotional heart of mine......that heart is always making me cry, so to protect it and make sure I'm far away from pride - I wear the garment that most people call shy..."

~ ~ ~

SON OF GOD
MARCH 31, 2013

"This marks the day that Jesus proved that He was right all along, that He was the Son of God, and the miracles He did were right never wrong......that He came from God Himself - no one other, to tell us something else He said to be true, that through Him we all can one day see the Father too..."

~ ~ ~

MIRROR IMAGE
APRIL 2, 2013

"Mirror image can be the same or opposites, we are both we ying and yang - you're outgoing I'm introverted, you've lived wild I've been sheltered, you're worldly, I'm practically a virgin.....but yet we're twins we have the same hands, same talents, same heart, same dreams and I believe, if you 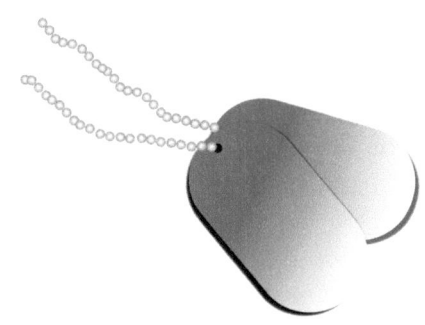 have anything to do with it, one day we'll have the same team..."

~ ~ ~

EXTRA MILE
MARCH 30, 2013

"Having someone compelled to be there for you, knowing they are there even when your back is turnt is a comfort very few get to feel, and very few have learned........someone with you on their mind throughout the day and when they wake feeling' your every joy and every ache........someone with that connection that loves you rich or poor, sick or healthy, that fights for you on every level.......very few get that experience, though some can fake it for a while, but there are those sent specifically for you, that don't mind walking that extra mile..."

~ ~ ~

SUBCONSCIOUS
MARCH 28,, 2013

"The mind is a funny thing so fragile yet powerful you will find, but yet so complicated at the same time......there is apart of the mind that you can't see, it's called the subconscious and its working on behalf of you controlling' everything you turn out to be.......it controls what you remember and controls every moving part that makes you sane, and what controls that part of the brain?......its everything you see, experience and choose to do, so be careful what you subject your eyes, ears and mind to - because what IT sees, thinks and carries-out is a reflection on you..."

~ ~ ~

YOUR LOVE IS SUPREME
SEPTEMBER 26, 2012

"You're love is supreme and its something I want to always feel, it wears me out sometimes when all night I feel the flow of your loving grow....... but it completes me and I'm proud to say, you're love-flow targets me hour by the hour in every single way.......your love is so supreme just the way it will always be, through time and space nothing stops me loving you - and

you loving me....... I won't ever ask God to take away this love cause it's real, realer than the Real Holyfield, yes you're love is supreme and its something I want to always feel..."

~ ~ ~

YOU ARE ART
MARCH 26, 2013

"You are more than an artist, YOU are art, everything about you is artistically done from the heart......I am more than a singer, I am Music, everything about me is artistically done from the heart - cause I am art....... we're lovers of fashion, showmanship, and the beat it satisfies our heart - because we - ARE art..."

~ ~ ~

THERE FOR YOU
MARCH 24, 2013

"A wife should always be with her husband to take care of his every need, their kids should always be with the wife so she can take care and feed....... a husband should always be with his family to protect and take care of their needs, this is the way it should be when you marry me..."

MY HEART
MARCH 23, 2013

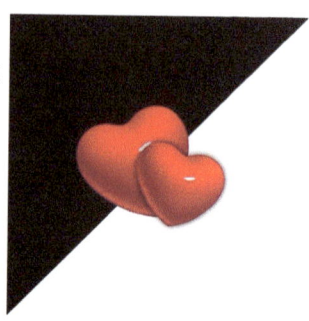

"Take my heart its all I have to give, take my love to keep you safe for as long as you live......free to live a life where you feel secure in love so you never roam, able to stay in love with that someone you can call your home.......those that love you will wish you well, and pray for you as I have been since the day I 'fell'..."

~ ~ ~
GOD'S TIMING
MARCH 22, 2013

"God gave to me on Christmas, 'His' Birthday, an amazing gift, exactly what I prayed for, but He did better than this....... He sent it in the form of a message something to do with a 10, what that meant I didn't know but knew it had to be very important........I'm sure it had to do with the love which He gave us as a gift, oh what a mighty God we have - His timing is perfect..."

~ ~ ~
THE APPLE OF MY EYE
MARCH 22, 2013

"Let love lead you - not desire, not want, not need, not fear, peer pressure or since of duty - for God will take care of those you'll see......He wants us to love, so let love be your guide, let love be the apple of your eye..."

~ ~ ~
NO REGRETS
MARCH 19, 2013

"I don't regret any words I've ever said for they came from a gentle heart God made, always wanting to help, love and uplift - the targeted ears of any fears someone gave......Shakespeare said 'I think you does protest too much' and there's an old saying 'the truth hurts' meaning if the words have weight, they'll stick in your brain and won't give you peace until the truth you face.......if there's no bases to what has been said, the words go in one ear and out the other - real fast.....though some of my feelings expressed in words fell short in the past, it's clear that I wouldn't change a thing I did or said cause it led to a love that will for every last..."

~ ~ ~

LIFE GOES ON
MARCH 18, 2013

"Each day when the sun rises it reminds us that life goes on, always another pair of arms, always someone to keep you warm...... I have found loving self is what gives you that solid ground so you can please, for when you love yourself there is no need to depend on anyone else to give you that love we all need......the mind is such a influential thing, if you don't screen what goes in you are liable to do just about anything........so guard your mind from what it hears and sees, for the mind is capable of acting out whatever it feels.........since my Love you are my other self, seems natural that I love you first and no one else......I have no doubt in my heart and Soul that you feel the same so I have no fears, and when I think about the depth of the love joy is what fills my tears........so each day when the sun rises I'm reminded of that love and what God brought us together for, to always have someone like the sun to keep our hearts safe and warm..."

~ ~ ~

GENIUS
MARCH 17, 2013

"I knew you were a genius from the start, not cause of what we see that you've done for I know the talents of one like you, cause I am a similar one - my talent is true.......but because of what's not seen with the public eye, I suspected from the start so on a pedestal I put you and here's why....you're one with so much awesome talent it gives you an edge, but your sweet and loving heart keeps you humble - not many know this - but I know cause I see what's in your head.......that alone will ensure your success, and your genius guarantees you will past any of life's test.....In your eyes I also see the ability to think of tons of things at once and not miss a beat, yet through it all my genius you find time to dedicate to Me..."

~ ~ ~
LOVE IN SILENCE
MARCH 14, 2013

"There is a lot to hear in silence, you hear things you didn't hear in the noise, you hear life as you've never heard it before.......you can almost hear the Master knocking' at your door, He is saying, "My child haven't spoken to you in a while".......and if you're quiet enough you will see He has  the answers to questions that you may say, He says through the birds, 'It will happen, I will make a way. I will take the wrong choices that I gave you freely since I created day, and I will turn them around for My Own's sake....... 'So don't worry,' He says through the morning sun 'never fear, cause I will never forsaken you, for you carried My tears'.....Yes there is a lot to hear in silence, you can see things you never saw before, like what you've done for me that not many can see or understand, except for the Master because the whole world is in His hands..."

~ ~ ~

METAMORPHOSIS
MARCH 13 2013

"I saw a metamorphosis from when you guys called that day, I knew it would happen cause God sent you my way.........that's what I told him that I was  shocked when he called said it must be a calling from a force that's much higher, for I was just about to retire.........but knowing that the call was a sign, saying don't pull out yet first help what is mine........and that's what I did and tried reaching out to each one of you so you can see, that God sent me to you, and He called you each His peach.......He gave me the plan, the direction, the words - He was an awesome Assist, for I have witness in you guys the greatest of metamorphosis..."

~ ~ ~

VOCAL DRAGON
MARCH 16, 2013

"Spitting your fire with that glorious voice of yours, melting hearts for your sound we adore........so powerful and deep a river flowing with heat, melting walls down, burning them down to the ground........that's your defense against ones who attack, your voice signaling that the Dragon is back..."

~ ~ ~

BRAVEHEART
MARCH 12, 2013

"It's amazing what's happenin', all because you dared to truly love, for some reason that makes me proud as if God touched us from above........everything imaginable has hit us to make it end, as I said in the beginning - I knew this would be, that it would take a man with a Brave heart to fight through - to get to me..."

~ ~ ~

FEMALE RATIO
MARCH 11, 2013

"When I was in the Navy male/female ratio was 1 to 5, maybe more, more men than women of that I am sure.......we had our pick and the guys were waiting inline, yet I decided to wait for the lifetime kind.......in civilian life it's just the reverse, too many females trying to tag a man of worth........men become spoiled and they don't see, that out of the 5 waiting inline, there's only one like Me..."

~ ~ ~

HATED ON
MARCH 10, 2013

"I been hated on by the same sex all my life - too big, too brown, big lips, big boobs, moles on my face, I once told you that when discussing myself that that is the case........which is why I said no

ex would let you take this cake, they would try to imitate me - to try and take my place.......then they will try and beat me down without explanation until I disappear, so no one will know what they got - they got from here.......so hating I'm use to - though this is the ultimate level you see, my only problem is you're not here with me..."

~ ~ ~

THE GIFT
MARCH 7, 2013

"We all have Godly gifts from birth that is maybe unlike someone else they wont understand your gift, and to you theirs will be amidst.......but what I tell my clients, and it's found to be true, if you put people in positions for personal reasons there will be no company growth you'll find, but push them where they are qualified and in time - watch them thrive..."

~ ~ ~

DREAM FOR US
MARCH 9, 2013

"A dream dreamt for us, started a chain reaction the moment our hearts touched.......no one can tell us why or how, but I don't care just as long as you are there.......we are doing what we have to do, to stay connected and true.......no matter what life throws

at us we don't question why, as long as in the end - there is still you and I..."

~ ~ ~

THROUGH MY BODY
MARCH 6, 2013

"Music flows through my body wherever I am, whenever I hear it no dance is the same....... it's the melody and the words that dictates my dance game, when I dance there is finally for me no pain........ I feel like dancing until the music stops and the world becomes mute, then I spend the rest of my time thinking of you..."

~ ~ ~

THE BAD
MARCH 5, 2013

"Something good comes out of something bad for those who work according to His will.......His plan is His plan no matter what the actions of man.......we lie and skim to get our way but we are just delaying that inevitable day.......He takes the bad and makes it good, to show us He cares, every bad event in my life as led me to an answer to my prayer........that's why when bad things happen to me, I stand still and I wait, for I know in time the Master will enact His will - and deal with the hate..."

HOPE
MARCH 4, 2013

"When it seems you can't give faith not even a mustard seed, there is hope, the coolest kind of dope...... keeps you uplifted and puts your mind on a better day, people gather around to hear your hope filled words loving what you have to say...... with hope in the dark you think of the sunrise in the morn, the clear skies once the rain stops, the fact that eventually you'll be back on top.......when it seems you can't give faith not another ounce for a better day, look at those that hold hope in you and realize it was there anyway..."

~ ~ ~

YOUR FACE
JANAURY 26, 2013

"Your happiness is all I want, to see your face light up with grace, that smile and personality shining through on your face.......that happiness for all the world to see, that look that says you're happy to see me......what ever you choose to do, just know I will always be loving you..."

~ ~ ~

ALL MINE
JANUARY 27, 2013

"Everyone wants to be loved for who they really are, to feel wanted and needed having someone not wanting to go too far.......someone you constantly long to kiss, someone even though its been hours you desperately miss......but after my friend left I wasn't looking to bond again, planned to live my life alone not even if he was a ten.......then your love came and snatched my heart.…....you said unlike my friend, you'd be there for me until the very end......I know you made that promise before, and I've been waiting at a similar door.......but maybe just maybe what I feel is saying this time, this time someone will open the door and say this one is all mine..."

~ ~ ~

JOURNEY
JANUARY 25, 2013

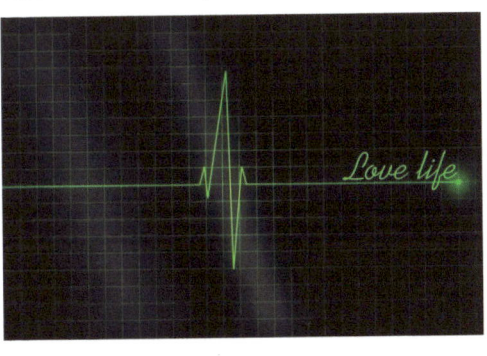

"I started this journey to Love aware - because of my past - that there would be a fight, I knew the past was there to teach me and was hoping I wouldn't need it to lead me.......unfortunately it had to be, maybe so you can really appreciate me.......it's my peaceful nature that makes me the target, I don't crave money or fame and some can't understand ....some see it as a weakness and try to go 'pound for pound' with me, what they don't know - what they can't see - you mess with me you have to deal with the God that's within me.......I started this journey to see if what I felt was real, what I found out is with you all wounds heal, I believe its because your Love is the 'real deal'..."

~ ~ ~

A ROSE
JANAURY 22, 2013

"One thing I think you know inside of me is a rose, the scent is sweet petals gentle and with your Love it will forever grow.......you know I'm gentle to the touch, that's why you surround me with your unconditional love........one thing about you I know for sure, you're a fearless tiger on the outside, what every woman is looking for......but on the inside you're precious and cute down to the core, offering love unconditional for the one that you adore..."

~ ~ ~

A-LIST
JANUARY 21, 2013

"You wanted to be current and now you are, to those that matter who means so much to you you're the best by far......to those unknown to what you do they just miss, but give it time my Love they'll see your name on the A-List..."

~ ~ ~

MY WINDOW
JANUARY 24, 2013

"Through my window to your Soul I see it everywhere I go, the first time I dared to look it was plain to see you were the male image of me.....amazed that you noticed me looking in, when you said my fair lady I've seen you before, but when?........I noticed in your Soul a restless one in deed, looking for someone who understands your needs - one willing to step back and let you be all you can be......your window to my Soul didn't see someone very old, but you saw the 16 yr-old girl within me yearning to be bold........you  thought I didn't notice the depth of your love for me, while you were trying to soak up every thought swimming in the depth of my sea........but I did notice though we had nothing to say, but what we saw through window's Soul still remains with us until today..."

~ ~ ~

LIFT SOMEONE ELSE
JANUARY 19, 2013

"Your dreams to achieve should depend on self or it should lift someone else.......never depend on the aide of someone for your dream to come true, only enlist others to help you......to say someone took your dream means it was theirs and never yours from the beginning, sometimes we impose our dreams upon another human being.......maybe you're too shy or too whatever to take advantage of God's blessing, but God would not have given the dream if He didn't think you could learn the lesson,......my dream won't satisfy you and yours I wont understand I just wont have a clue, God gives us all dreams we can accomplish alone with just you two.......He's just waiting for you to ask Him to take you to fore fill your dream, most just sit waiting for the ocean to split before they make a move it seems......Your dreams to achieve should depend on self with the help of a hired team, not stealing a free ride on someone's wings......our dream Love is a life together without worry, to maintain a friendship by any means necessary..."

~ ~ ~

BECOME WE
JANUARY 18, 2013

"If you have to push your way into a person's life its not the place for you to be hanging onto, when someone 'makes' a place for you its an indication they sincerely want you.......that place I talk about is not the space that surrounds a persons body, that space I talk about is in that person's heart where my Love is hiding.....the only place people can't evade without your say, that's why with drama and confusion away I try to stay......if you have to buy your way in or get there by fear, it's not a place for you my dear.......cause you're only there for a second in the scope of time, a place where no one cares to venture out to find.....its the heart and the thoughts of a person is where I want to be, cause that's the closest you could ever be to someone - the place where you stop being I but become we..."

~ ~ ~

YOUR BIGGEST FAN
JANUARY 5, 2013

"Its safe to say I'm your biggest fan, your biggest supporter in all the land.......you answer me even before I have something you say, its safe to say you complete me in every way....... Id like to make sure I can do the same for you. the one who changed me from a singular Being to two........Its safe to say I'm your biggest fan, the biggest supporter of the guy who has my right hand..."

WITH YOU
JANUARY 3 2013

"Life with you sounds exciting when I think of 'it living life a different way, I get scared cause I don't want to loose you to 'it' not for a day.......pleasures of the world could never entice me to take my eyes off you, I'm rich beyond belief as long as there is me and there is you........my pleasure lies in looking into your face, that of someone who is pleased with my taste.......life with you sounds exciting I look forward to the walk, just to see your face everyday and listen to you talk..."

~ ~ ~

KEEP THE LIE
JANUARY 7, 2013

"Some people live in their own created worlds called a lie, you're not welcome unless you keep the lie alive.......I choose to live in reality what ever the case may be, good or bad because truth is what sets me free......only those willing to except reality get my attention, because in my reality a lie don't get no mention........some people live in their own created worlds called a lie, you're not welcome in it unless you keep the lie alive…"

NEW YEAR
JANUARY 1, 2013

"1st day of a New Year for you it means a new home new lover with more hugging and experiences you've dreamt would be, this new year for me means unlimited possibilities that God let me see........He already gave me the Christmas gift I spoke of when I prayed, He even allow me to see the answer to a question hidden behind a close door in a fresh way........He did it in a way that connected to a conversation we had one day, and the message was with certainty everything was going to be OK......I woke up with a smile on my face, not from the love you give, but because of HIS Grace......its the 1st day of a New Year for you that means all injustices are behind, as we watch Christ turn plain water into quality wine........ He will turn the year of The Snake and it will be gone, replaced with last year - the miracle year of The Dragon..."

~ ~ ~

PLAY DAY
DECEMBER 31 2012

"Everyday will be play day, so use to having fun we won't have time for drama......everyday you'll be able to play with me, what a life it will be......me loving you and you loving me..."

~ ~ ~
I WILL FOLLOW
JANUARY 2, 2013

"All my life I been a leader but didn't want to in my marriage though, but sometimes in life that's the way it may have to go.........never felt comfortable following anyone but God, He is the one that really knew the desires of my heart........but in a marriage I have a need to follow - if you can understand, led by a loving, kind and providing kind of man........yes, I'm a leader cause in life its hard to trust anyone to be true, but for some reason Love - I feel safe following you..."

YOUR LOVE TEACHES ME
DECEMBER 21, 2012

"You be my teacher and I will be yours, each day we reach another level no one will keep score ......and when the teaching is over and the learning is done, we retire and spend the rest of our days becoming as one...."

~ ~ ~
THE HEAT
DECEMBER 20, 2012

"Your love is the heat in the midst of a winter storm, you can take on any form.........you're a walking evolution when its time you know what to do, always creatively changing into a brand new you........your love is the chill in the midst of a heat wave, you're my fly breeze sending many scents my way..... ...what a life filled with endless possibilities, a Rock-N-Roll love that the world loves to see.........your love is the heat in the midst of a winter storm, reaching through time and space to keep me safe and warm..."

THE WORLD NEEDS LOVE
DECEMBER 19, 2012

"What the world needs is Love, the kind you give to your little baby boys and girls, the kind that's not of this world.......what the world needs is Love, the kind that's given from All Mighty God above, the kind you just can't get enough of.........Love in its most purest form is when its returned from a place deep within, especially when it puts you on another level than what was given..........what the world needs is Love, the kind that makes people protect and help until the world think you've lost your mind, the kind that is more valuable than any treasure you can find - the kind of love like yours and like mine..."

~ ~ ~

YOUR SPIRITUAL ROLE
DECEMBER 18, 2012

"God's children all have a role to play in life, and some of our roles are not so nice....... but if we are to fight to protect the Light sometimes we have to pick up the gun, the sword and the knife.......to protect a love one we must fight hate as if its an everyday thing, pick up the sword and put our life on the line - do just about any-

thing.........God's children all have to play their part in life that's the way it goes, even Jesus had a role - to die, rise again to prove through Him we can save our Souls..."

~ ~ ~

A MUSICAL
DECEMBER 17, 2012

"Our home will be like a musical from sun up to sunset, those that visit us will dance around giving a performance we will never forget........our home with be full of laughter, silliness and love, the kind that brings peace of mind like the sight of a dove.......our home will be full of sexiness, romance and affection because I act like that, the kind of home when you're away you cant wait to get back........our home will be like a musical from sun up to sunset, full of surprises and far off places and people I've never met ..."

~ ~ ~

PLEASES ME
DECEMBER 16, 2012

"Your love pleases me so deep is it if I bleed you bleed, your love feeds me keeps me full so that there is no one else I need.........your body teases me I need it near where it needs to be, spend the day me catering to you as you cater to me...........it will take a life time for me to get bored everyday will be brand new, each day I will find something I love that's different and fly in you.........your love pleases me so deep its like this, when you are not here you are deeply missed….so much so when I see you next I guarantee this, there's not one place I wouldn't kiss..."

~ ~ ~

I CAN BE ME
DECEMBER 15, 2012

"With you I will finally be able to be just a lady, for the first time in my life I will wear only one hat, that of your one and only baby.....With you I wont have to worry about bringing in the bread, and for the first time in my life someone will appreciate the "nighties" I wear to bed.......With you I can be the artist I was born to be, for the first time in my life I will be able to be the real me..."

~ ~ ~

~ ~ ~
MY KING
DECMBER 13, 2012

"You're the lord of the ring, you're my everything.......I don't fear loving you until you say "when," will do it forever and then do it again......that's what God gave me you for - to love and love - then love you some more......you're my king, I hear you in everything when I sing..."

~ ~ ~
BOY MEETS GIRL
DECEMBER 14, 2012

"That age old story boy meets girl, then everything changes in their world....... they are from different sides of the street, neither side seems to want the two to meet.......that age old story told as 'Romeo and Juliet", one of those tales you'll never ever forget....... the struggle for this love set off so many fires, it caused everyone to go all unwired.......why does love get such a bad rap, why isn't it served with a endless 'flow of understanding' tab....... its that age old story boy meets girl, the combining of two different worlds..."

~ ~ ~

THE WORLD STAGE
NOVEMBER 20, 2012

"The world is a stage where we are all players, but the casting director is God and the audience are your haters.......your role and the scripts' direction is based on your choices in life, from the time the 'director' says ACTION and you pick up the mic.......my role is named Music, I'm the sound-track to the play, I sing you the melody to explain what the characters are trying to say.........the world is a stage where we are all players, just doing what we do, before an audience of haters........as you play your part in life's play are you staying true, and what is your role so far saying about you..."

~ ~ ~

THE TRAIN
NOVEMBER 19, 2012

"I hear the click-a-dee-clack of the tracks, wonder if that's his train coming back..........when it left I remember its warm caboose, its windows - the eyes to its inner truth........I hear the click-a-dee-clack of the tracks, wonder if that's his train coming back........its one I think I'd like

to ride, ride it for life to the other side......I hear its whistle now warning its almost here, I can feel my Love's on board - finally someone to love me without fear..."

~ ~ ~

TAKE A BITE
NOVEMBER 18, 2012

"Take a bite of me I've saved a piece just for you, you see..........cause I knew you'd arrive hungry for me......... take a sip of my tea, I've kept it sweet and warm.........cause I knew you'd arrive thirsty as a sailor that's been out in salt water seas too long........I've prepared a main course meal, don't worry Love I'll keep your belly filled ......Take a bite of me I've saved some desert, take a bite of it, it wont hurt..........cause I knew you'd arrive just in time, to feed me your love as I've fed you mine..."

~ ~ ~

DIFFERENT FACE
NOVEMBER 16, 2012

"They say male and female numbers don't add up, that some will be left with no one to take - no Soul mate.......I say numbers are just as they need to be, that their Soul mate may be too young, in college, too far away to see.........they may be a member of another race, religion or someone with an old familiar face.........if we just take off

our blinders of the superficial to see the heart and Soul and not just the pretty face, look deeper to see the things that can't be replaced like their honor, their upbringing, or their degree of Spiritual faith..........they say male and female numbers don't add up, that the monogamy way of life is so old ....that males should have more than one mate, and women should take that as the case..........I say your Soul mate is out there, I've had two in one life time, so I know everyone has at least one that they can find............someone that compliments them, brings peace of mind and loves deeply their face, someone that can never ever be replaced - someone with a totally different face..."

~ ~ ~

MASTER YOU SERVE
NOVEMBER 14, 2012

"They say being bad feels good, I say it depends on where you from in your hood..........what makes you feel good is a testament to your character, defines what you been hoping for what pushes you further......Me, being bad would mean a sleepless night, waking up thinking something's just not right.........for some with a heart dark as black coal, being bad means 'for-sale' is their Soul......they say being bad feels good for those that have the nerve, I say it just shows what Master you serve..."

THE MASTERS PLAN
NOVEMBER 13, 2012

"People talk about karma cause God say you reap what you sow, like they're sinless with no room to grow........karma is the result of what you 'give' to the world you see, good or bad you get it back 'organically' ....but those talking of karma cant wait for nature they create perils to try and pierce each others armor, like 'their' name is God or even Karma........but if they leave things to God put their opinions in a song, they may find out that they judged wrong........ that God wouldn't have allowed a reprimand, because what happen was a part of the Masters plan..."

~ ~ ~

TEN FEET TALL
MARCH 3, 2013

"I was obsess with height, prayed for someone much taller to feel safe to hold me tight.......but God has shown me through life experiences and I think He's right, that height is not physical - as beauty is not.......height is of character statue in life, through the number of people that love and respect you that catch you when you fall, so even though you're just an inch taller than I, to me Love - you're 10 feet tall..."

~ ~ ~

MY PASSIONS
FEBRUARY 16, 2013

"I get my passions not from when others hate against me or from revenge hitting its mark.......but my passion comes from love, the love of writing, the love of song, the love of nature, the love of dance - that gives my passion its spark..........my success is not measured by material things gained, fame, popularity and such, my success is waking up doing what I love, being able to use the gifts I received from God above........"revenge is mine" say the Lord, for only He knows the hearts of man.......a manager says you're not doing your job you need to be fired, is he being mean or trying to spark something in you to reach higher........someone sees a mean streak in someone and tells the target beware, is that mean-spirited or an action of someone who the target they care.........I get my passion not from when others hate or in seeking revenge cause that kind of passion is short lived, I get my passion from love - cause that kind of passion never ends..."

~ ~ ~

LOVE RUNS THE WORLD
FEBURARY 4, 2013

"Takes Love to run the world, that's the only thing the world needs, for boy or for girl.......Love makes the pain go away, Love is the light that brightens up your dark day, Love is what makes me stay.......whatever the future holds for us two, just always know I'll always be loving you .....because Love is the cure for all that ails you, Love is what makes one person out of two...... Love is a power that moves one to do things out of compassion, its the substance that is forever lasting.....takes Love to run the world, in it you can find that one priceless pearl........in Love you can beat any negative forced man can make, in Love the underdog becomes the brave..."

~ ~ ~

FILLS MY HEART
FEBRUARY 2, 2013

"Fills my Soul with joy, that you are a man now and no longer a boy.......you look at life in a different way, your thoughts are on family a warm home for the children to play........now when your travels take you from this country to that, there's no need to look for someone to care cause my love for you is always there........fills my Soul with happiness, that you need me to fill your circle to make it complete, that's why you will always have a devoted lover in me..."

~ ~ ~
YOUR SCENT
FEBURARY 1, 2013

"I hear the wind as it's going by, making the violin strings sound out in a cry, making the flute whistle and sing, making the horn blow and do its thing...... here comes that wind its power is headed my way, listen close you can even hear what it has to say......the wind is as gentle as can be, as everyday it brings your scent to me..."

FOREVER CHANGED
JANUARY 31, 2013

"No matter how life will be one thing is true, I won't worry cause I will be always following you........my hero my answer from above, you're my ying, my home - the one I can forever love.......yes, no matter what life brings one thing is true, my life forever changed the day I met you..."

~ ~ ~

YOUR LIGHT
JANUARY 30, 2013

"You're my light and I am yours, so bright it can be seen through any closed door...... we warm each other and brighten each others way, before we go off and start our day.......isn't it nice to know and to believe, that whatever happens in life our light will always be..."

~ ~ ~

A PLACE FOR HOPE
JANUARY 29, 2013

"Hope - when every dark night changed with the morning light, hope, that which makes everything bad alright......Hope - it chases fears away, is a magnet for positivity - what more can I say.....Hope - like the rivers' never ending stream, that which has no death it seems.....Hope - when you're sad it brightens up your day, its that smile you see on a precious baby's face......Hope - lives within me and it lives within you, a place you can trust - its a place where you can always go to for Love..."

~ ~ ~

BE ALL THAT YOU CAN BE
JANUARY 28, 2013

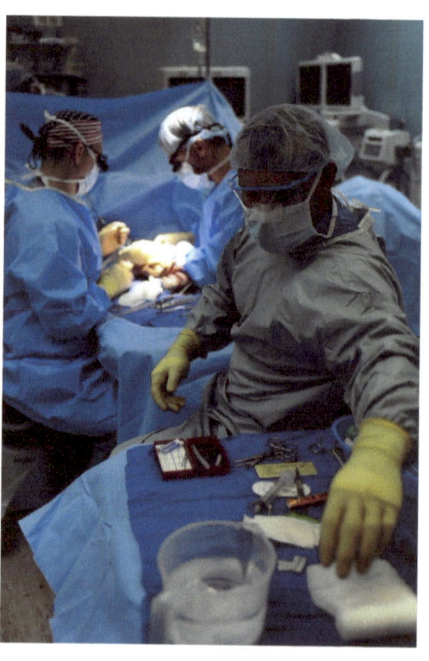

"I've had a long and prestigious career, done so many wonderful things forever I can share.......like my mother before me she with no High School degree she became a Surgical Tech - I guess you can say she won, she ended up with the respect of so many open heart surgeons.......it was implanted in me to strive for perfection, my mom said anything less and you're just not using your blessing.......you've had a long and prestigious career, done so many wonderful things that forever you can share.......Love, you will always be a diamond that everyone can see, you who was always determined to be all that you could be..."

~ ~ ~

WARMED BY YOUR SUN
MARCH 8, 2013

"The sun seems brighter today even though its not that hot, reminds me of the light in your heart, bright enough to made your head drop.......maybe that's why the world flocks to you, the warmth can turn grey skies to blue...... its what I see in your eyes - the portal to your Soul, your love for me - like the sun, will never grow old..."

~ ~ ~

GIVE IN LOVE
DECEMBER 4, 2012

"It feels good to give making people happy when they're sad, a simple smile to brighten up someone's day ....giving love to the depressed, lonely and even the bad, for some its the only thing of worth they will ever have.......to them there is not much you can say, so give a hug until the negativity goes away.......it feels good to give that you can believe, the Bible says its more bless to give than it is to receive........accepting love, you know you should, gives someone else a chance to feel good...."

~ ~ ~

MY HEART BEAT
DECEMBER 3, 2012

"Can you hear it, its the sound of my heart, beating to the rhythm that began when we

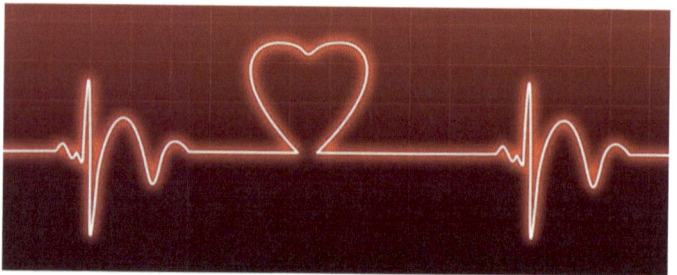

started.......Can you hear it, the sound indicating you've captured my heart, it beats so loud since the day we parted......Can you hear it, its the sound of my heart, it skipped a beat when you showed you're never too far.......Can you hear it, its the sound of my heart that you own, its beating the same over and over again - " you're my heart, you're my home..."

~ ~ ~

TO THE LIMIT
DECEMBER 2, 2012

"Take it to the limit and when you can't go no more, have faith in God the One who can open any door........take me to the limit, wherever you go, there I will be with the only one strong enough to fully love Me........take it to the limit and when you get there don't turn back looking at your faults, God wants your eyes on Him who is living deep within your heart........take me to the limit, I have no fears, as long as you are with me to wipe away my tears..."

~ ~ ~

I AM SHE
NOVEMBER 29, 2012

"Take me as I am...I am she .....I wear no mask - I am the only character cast......take me as I am...I am she .....take me and my flaws - I never let them define that which you re-gard......I am she....a. smiler, feeler, singer, jokester, good deed toaster.....I am she.....take me as I am, I wear no mask, I am the only character cast....I am she"

THE BOSS
NOVEMBER 28, 2012

"With God its never too late, even on our death bed, our Lord gives us one more chance to give and not take.......one more chance to catch the repent train to His Heavenly gates - its never too late.......one more chance to respect His way of life, one lived in love - Its never too late........even when it seems all hope is lost there's one more chance to do what pleases God - no matter what the cost.....'cause at the end of the day He is still the Boss..."

~ ~ ~

I AM MUSIC
NOVEMBER 27, 2012

"I sing because I'm happy, I sing because that's just Me, I sing when I'm not talking, and I sing when I'm sleep........I dance because it moves me, when I dance it sets me free, when the rhythm hits me I can't help but move my legs and feet....... when I hear music it gets hard for me to keep still, when I feel the beat my body has its own will ...... I sing because that's my purpose, its what makes my heart tick, I sing always deep in my Soul - that's why God calls me Music..."

CAN'T BE REPLACED
NOVEMBER 26, 2012

"Wish I was there to wipe the sweat from your face, trace your lips and whisper how your love can't be replaced.........wish I was there to hang on your arm, laugh as you hold me back when I hear my favorite song........when you're working I'm there to protect your personal belongings, and when you're here I fill your every longing........wish I was there to wipe the sweat from your face after you've come from the stage where you have been, then cool you down with kisses and set there while you talk of your day and I tentatively listen..."

~ ~ ~

AGE IS A NUMBER
NOVEMBER 25, 2012

"Age is a number of years lived, maturity is something you learn to give.........with matters of the heart its age-blind you see, its only concern is the connection between you and me..........one day we found that loversflow, we jumped in not carrying where that river goes........age is a number of years lived, love is something you learn to give.......with matters of the heart we're all needy you see, we need constant attention from someone who loves us deeper than anyone can believe..."

~ ~ ~

ALL I NEED
NOVEMBER 23 2012

"Your Love is all I need, it makes me feel I can do anything........your Love is the wind beneath my wings, it makes me fly so high all I do all day is sing......your Love is my comic relief when life takes a seri-  ous turn. it makes me smile for no reason I've learn.....now that I found you I know my purpose was to bring you that music - you know, and I know why that love-energy is so powerful........powerful enough to give me strength to take chances, give me the willingness to just dance, dance, dance.......your Love is all I need - its supreme, it makes me feel I can do just about anything..."

~ ~ ~

I SEE YOU
NOVEMBER 22, 2012

"I can feel you needing me for company just someone to be with, I see you Love, I see you - I see right through your eyes I must admit - but I'd share your burdens and walk in your shoes in a minute........I can feel your pride because right or wrong your choices was intended to bring you closer to your babies, I see you........In the future Love your history's struggles will be overshadowed and all that we will see is what a wonderful dad you turned out to be..."

~ ~ ~
MY MJ
NOVEMBER 21, 2012

"You're Michael Jackson with all the smooth moves, fly styles, people skills, creative genius - a rare jewel.......the world is craving you again they want to get hooked, knew you'd be a master of the same artistic book........you're Michael Jackson in every since of the word, your power personality gives trends its birth.........so great are your skills, any imperfections are concealed, hidden deep in your natural sex appeal ....you're Michael Jackson the man with the tender heart, who needs someone always with you to protect it from falling apart..."

~ ~ ~

STARTED WITH A BLANK CANVAS
NOVMBER 11, 2012

"The world started with Art, a blank canvas started it all.........before it was touched by the wars and rumors of war, before jealousy, hate and judgment debates......there was a blank canvas that started with clear blue skies and breath-taking landscapes.......with the stroke of a brush the painter made the crystal clean river streams..........sunrises and unforgettable sunsets more beautiful than any dream.........the painter gets passionate when he paints the oceans running deep, the green grass to protect our feet........The world is Art clearly seen in the creatures created by the painter, they serve the painters greatest design to make the painting so sweet, man and his mate - and now the painting is complete..."

~ ~ ~

DREAMS, GOD'S PHONE LINE
NOVEMBER 6, 2012

"Dreams allude me but I know they're there used by people everyday, God's private communication line to show us the way..........so I rely on nature like birds to sing me God's melody, through the people He put in my life to dance me to where I need to be.......Dreams are also what we accomplish in life, the accumulation of struggles, challenges and triumphs after many fights.......Blessed are those with the ability to Dream, what a gift to be able to communicate with the Most High King..."

~ ~ ~

THERE I GO
NOVEMBER 4, 2012

"Like ying and yang, black and white, fast and slow we're two pieces of a whole, where ever you be - there I go.....we're like grapes and wine, like now is to time we got something that you just can't easily define..."

~ ~ ~

CHERRY WINE
NOVEMBER 1, 2012

"The heart, the heart, the heart is where its found if you looking for love, the emotion that knows no bounds make us forget what was..........take a look and you will see how you, my Love, lives deep within me.........my heart is your bedroom, my eyes are the door, my lips are the key that keeps you wanting more........your heart, your heart, your heart is where I'm found when you need someone around.......your heart is my backbone, your eyes is all in me that's kind, your lips taste like sweet cherry wine..."

~ ~ ~

BACK TO ME
OCTOBER 31, 2012

"I hear clicks, its an instrument I can't define, sounds like the clicks of women heels, or drums stick fighting for the last meal.......I hear clicks so sassy makes my body pop, its an instrument I can't define, sounds like the click of tap heel shoes, dancing their way back to you..."

~ ~ ~

JOB WELL DONE
OCTOBER 28, 2012

"The chance to work with the famous SisQo and his partners Dru Hill, when I got the call I knew it was a dream come true, even though I thought my days of pressure-cooking was through, I took the task for a chance to work with you.......I took the assignment cause the timing said it was God who really asked, cause my time consulting was to be a thing of the past.......most sincerely it was the need that I heard from my friend who I adored, he was a person I'd do anything for.......so what do I do, what can I say to show them the way to get through some doors, on my knees I went like with everything I do everyday, I prayed that God would show me the way.........that way was what I told them in a strategy they should do, I tried taking off their blinders with strategic observations so they can see the way I saw too........management said pave the way, fill up those holes so we can find our way to the gold.......the chance to work with the famous SisQo and his partners Dru has been a testament of my faith in God, an example of how I walk in Love, and it proved that my walk is true......still, I'd do it again cause it made me the lucky One meeting you.........I did my job and I can see in a big way you've all touched the Son, I know it cause this morning God said, 'My child, job well done'..."

~ ~ ~
PICTURE OF YOU
OCTOBER 24, 2012

"Whenever I get homesick missing my family 3,000 miles away, I find a picture of you and magically I'm home like I never missed a day......Whenever I miss the hometown seasons the North Ave drive, taking me from west to east side.........I find a picture of you and I see home, seeing only the best in life, the worst is gone.......no matter where I go, whatever parts of the world unknown, as long as I have you with me, I'm home, sweet home..."

~ ~ ~
HEAVEN IN YOUR EYES
OCTOBER 22 , 2012

"Heaven is in your eyes the sun in your smile, to see them again I'd walk for miles and miles......for inside you there's my hope, a peace, and a man that looks just like me......Heaven is in your eyes perfection in your smile, I plan to make sure they stay there - for a long, long while..."

~ ~ ~

FOLLOWING YOUR LEAD
OCTOBER 13, 2012

"Your love guides me, as I follow your lead with every piece of strength I have inside of  me........your love is my light illuminating my way, building my trust up so that I'm able to follow you every single day.......because for what we had to endure just cause we want to love each other a little bit more.......Its the evidence that anyone willing to see can believe, that there is nothing that can distinguish that red flame that love has ignited inside of you and inside of me..."

~ ~ ~

BEAT OF THE DRUM
OCTOBER 5, 2012

"I hear drums beats starting soft then rising loud as if announcing a coming, could it be the ending or beginning of something?.......I hear the symbols tinkering a melody, great sounds announcing what we are about to see........I hear drums beating from the flow of the sticks pounding as if The King is here, could it be a message from God saying don't worry my child there is nothing to fear...........what a power those drums have when they sound off I still hear the beats, fits perfect with my heart song and its because of the love you bring to me..."

~ ~ ~

HERE WITH ME
OCTOBER 5, 2012

"You are around the world and yet you are here with me, you don't have to say a word, but yet what you say I can see........the real and the mental brings your warm body next to me, your passionate love allows me to be there when you need.......you are around the world and yet you are here with me, the real and the mental as you can see..."

YOUR SIDE KICK
OCTOBER 1, 2012

"You take my breath away the love you give me everyday, can't put a price on it, can't give it away cause its mine - its custom made finer than wine......you keep my heart beating with this invisible bond between us two, the sight of you always turns my grey skies to blue.......try to take what we have try to block us so we can't see, and my love becomes a tiger, a Jr Ali and me? I become his side kick, the legendary Bruce Lee..."

~ ~ ~

LOVE YOUR GUITAR BEAT
AUGUST 17,, 2012

"I hear that guitar scratching a funky sound, that guitar just keep rocking my body down to the ground.......I hear a beat like someone knocking at my door, persistently playing moving my body to the core........I hear that guitar screaming not sad but like a kid at play, jumping around enjoying the life that God has made.........that's how your love is its funky always rocking with a beat that would past any test, a reminder that when man says no God can say yes..."

~ ~ ~

YOU DID IT
AUGUST 14, 2012

"Could it be you did it, united people that were once a wall trying to prevent your red Love-flow from reaching me, from being free to love who you want - and just be free........could it be you did it brought peace to the collective with your wisdom and your loving heart, ensuring that everyone will play  apart of this miracle that brings us all to the light from the dark.......your Soul speaks to mine before it even speaks to me, your the master of my ship sail - the captain of my rough seas..."

~ ~ ~

YOU'VE NEVER LET GO
AUGUST 13, 2012

"You've never let go of my hand in no way, not since my first vision of you reaching out for me that day......... though you were blocked at every turn, still you never let go you took it and you learned.......you never let go of my hand not even for a day, you just found the strength and found another way.......all those smoking mirrors to make you seem like something you not, are not getting me down I won't give up the fight........ like superman I see right through now, its crystal clear blue now...........you've never let go of my hand always reaching out for me, helping me to hold on making our love grow, that's why I see through the BS and I pray that you know - that your hand I will never let go..."

~ ~ ~
PRICELESS LOVE
SEPTEMBER 22, 2012

"They can't afford what we got can't buy it for nothing, they can't afford what we got it can't be brought not even by a king...........cause love is priceless yet its free, the most priceless thing to possess like the love from you that I see..."

~ ~ ~
THE FUTURE IS OURS
SEPTEMBER 21, 2012

"The future is ours to make as we wish, we have the gift of free-will to choose any of life's delicious gifts.......the future is ours a destiny given to everyman, in the future there's togetherness cause that's our destiny God has planned.....fighting life's battles hand in hand is how it will always be, through each other's eyes is how we will see.......because one moment in time sparked a love so true, and now the future is unrecognizable and everyday is brand new..."

YOUR LOVE BRINGS PEACE
SEPTEMBER 19, 2012

"You brought peace to my life, when it gets a lil' scary I hold on to you all night........you brought sense to my life again. now when I need a friend I talk to you - and you listen..."

~ ~ ~

FILLS THE VOID
SEPTEMBER 17, 2012

"Only you can fill the void - that empty space, can't substitute you for someone you can't be replaced..........I don't know how to cook what ingredients to put or how long to keep it on the heat, but I do know without you by my side my recipe is not complete.........they say no person should complete you that you should be whole from the start, I say if that's so why did God create a life-mate 'til death do you they part.........only you can fill the void - be my home, no one sends me that energy - its like nothing can go wrong..."

~ ~ ~

SUPERMAN
SEPTEMBER 15, 2012

"I'm not superwoman, but he is my superman, and to pay back the love he gives, I'll do all that I possibly can........I'm not wonder woman, but he is my Spiderman scaling tall buildings to get to me, diving into the unknown just to rescue me, that's why like Spiderman's mask, I will never leave, like Spiderman is to trouble

- he can always count on me.......I'm not superwoman, but one thing for sure you can bet, like superwoman I will always be here protecting his happiness..."

~ ~ ~
LOVE'S ENERGY
SEPTEMBER 12, 2012

"Love is an energy felt between two unseen by the naked eye, but felt by those in tuned..........love is a life force that exist between two that connects them in a special way, never dying even after their dying day........Love is our lifeline to our creator it fills us up when we're hungry, quenches our thirst when thirsty, holds our hand when in need of company, has our back when we need a friend, heals us when we're sick - the energy it spills out is something no one can resist........our love energy held us to-  gether without us knowing, it told faith to try again, it told hope keep searching - never end.........love is the energy felt between us too unseen by the naked eye, but felt by those in tune........ love is the force that exist between us connecting us in a special way, never dying even after our dying day..."

~ ~ ~

YOU STAND OUT IN A CROWD
SEPTEMBER 9 2012

"Your sweetness tops my list, a list of things I can not miss........you stand out in the crowd of posts on my social pages I see, like your eyes stood out when you looked at me..........though you can be hard on the world when you turn in my direction, your words become honey sweet always for my protection......... you appreciate all that I do for you I'm your angel, Heaven sent me to you Mr. Tiger Print.........so to the pretenders of my lovers heart, there is no doubt I can tell you two apart............like the difference in your words - yours from the Light theirs from the dark, one is full of love and the other full of bark..."

ANIMAL LOVE
SEPTEMBER 8, 2012

"We're all animals living to consume our next meal, our next lay, our next thrill...what puts humans at the top of the pyramid of the life-chain link?, we can chose and the others are all instinct....we're all animals living each day to find our next prey, you're the tiger, me the lion - you want to play?..."

~ ~ ~

SAIL WITH ME
SEPTEMBER 7, 2012

"Take a sail with me there is so much I need to see but can't take the sail unless you're next to me........take a sail with me the ocean breeze makes me feel so alive - gets me in the right mood to take that dive……..we have so many cheering us on I think the world can see that being together is why we were born,.......whether we're together tied by the Soul, by the hip, by the Spirits' chain or the connection we have in our hearts and brain …….one thing is for sure now that we found each other we will never be apart never feel unloved, because we been favored with a special gift from the Master of love..."

REMEMBER MUSIC
AUGUST 1, 2012

"Remember the music when things get you down, there's truth in it, it puts the light in any frown.......remember the music every lil' piece, its in your being there's so much more to unleash.......I'm told I was music from conception until today, Maybe that's why we keep meeting its inevitable in every way.......remember Music when things get you down, Music's by your side forever found..."

~ ~ ~

LOVE FOUND ME
JULY 30, 2012

"Wasn't looking for love but yet love found me you see, I was 100% with no needs but yet you complete me.......guess that's how real love deals, why its something you have to feel.....wasn't thirsty for love making, yet your love I crave, wasn't stressed for company, yet yours is now part of my maze........guess that's why its something no one can see, why its something you have to feel and believe.."

~ ~ ~

MY BACK
JULY 27, 2012

"You bring the light to my darkness, you make me smile no matter how hard life is that's why no matter where you are at, I know you will always have my back..."

~ ~ ~

NEVER LETTING GO
JULY 26, 2012

"Never letting go no matter how the time flows, I'm never letting go no matter how hard the pressure grows.........never letting go no matter what obstacles may come my way, I'm never letting go no matter what they all say.......never giving up on you no matter what people do, I'm never letting go of us two.......through all the ups and downs that life demands, I'm never letting go cause its all part of God's grand plan..."

~ ~ ~

DAVID AND GOLIATH
JULY 23, 2012

"What a wonder Love is, it makes you David brave enough to fight Goliath, makes you believe there's a chance, the joy makes you wild enough to dance when others say you can't.........what a wonder Love is it gives you peace when hate is near, makes your journey something you don't really ever fear, because you know Love is always near.........what a wonder Love is it brings the light/ truth to a dark over cast day, its bright enough to last until our dying day..........what a wonder your Love is to me, did you know with your Love we can handle anything..."

~ ~ ~

TEST OF TIME
JULY 20, 2012

"Time's too short, all we have is now, now to love, now to be happy, now to be all we can be......cause time's to short, all we have is choice, to choose to give, to choose to take, to choose to be real or to be fake.......but what we don't have is perfection, we can only strive for the best, for at the end of your life, this whole thing is just God's test..."

~ ~ ~

LOVE STREAMS
JULY 19, 2012

"Waking up with you on my mind is like waking up thankful for a treasure un-found...when I met you your gleam wasn't quit shinning, your smooth edges were chipped, you were a gem no one seemed to  want to mess with....then your love for me started shinning through, thanks to the changes you made within you, making you fully in tacked, and as I predicted your youth is even back..... .waking up feeling you deep in my Soul is like waking up realizing the fire we share has made me gold, because of you I'm shinning so nice, that now it seems they're calling me your ice....from this day forward no matter what the day brings I know the love we share has made you an every flowing love stream..."

~ ~ ~

THE KEYS
JULY 17, 2012

"I hear the piano keys, tapping down the marble street, telling me you almost here follow me……..I can hear the piano keys' sweet sound like bells, leading me to you and I see the tale of what it tells - tells of a love so true, nothing on this earth could every replace you for me, and me for you….I hear the piano keys, making me get up out my seat, making me twirl carelessly, thinking of the day when you are forever with me...."

~ ~ ~

EVIL USES GODS WORDS
JULY 10, 2012

"Words, unlike a physical hit, stays with you until your mind is able to dismiss……..words form thoughts and thoughts form actions, that's why the devil's favorite tool is words used that aren't factual - used in a way to create a harmful reaction…….sometimes hate is wrapped up in words of grandeur, dress as scripture, coming to you as God's mission….but this is how you determine if the words are that of the righteous, used as tools of the Lord, if the words come from one known to tell the truth, if they make your haters voices become mute………..if the words make you love someone other than yourself, if the words are minus venom - words that reach out' to someone to help…"

~ ~ ~

REAL LOVE IS A WINNER
JULY 9, 2012

"Face the fact, real love is where its at...wanna get high, just look your lover in the eye, if its real, here's the deal - cloud9 is what you will feel……..face the fact, trust is a must between us...wanna love to last forever, if its real here's how you must live - your total focus is what you must give...just the thought of you - your eyes, your lips, your shape, your attention - has me turning from a victim into a 'winner"…"

~ ~ ~

ANGEL FOR YOU
JULY 7, 2012

"You so sweet to your angel but it seems, though she came here to help you she can be heard whispering 'please don't leave me'……..she so sweet to you your her precious jewel you make life seem brand new, that you're often heard whispering back, 'don't you leave me too'……..you so easy to love, that's why you're a winner, like me you're about the truth, cause your love's not a pretender……..if you're riding you warn them let them know, if your devoted then you let it show …..and oh how you're so funny to me, need laughter in my life at all times, you provide it with the heart of lion…..you're a warrior under fire, yet still sweet enough to share that light you have from up Higher…….you so easy to love, that's why you're a winner, like me you are about 'love' and what is 'just' that's why after all the attacks - we still believe in us..."

~ ~ ~

WE DON'T HAVE TO CALL
JULY 6, 2012

"My special Love, such a wild child that grew up so quick -

cause of the love he found...my special baby, so sexually charged my sexy guiding star.... my special love, my sweet gift from above, the whole world will soon see , that you were meant to be with me...as the sun rises and then as it falls, that's how it is with us - working so close - we don't even have to call..."

~ ~ ~

RARE DIAMOND
JULY 4, 2012

"Your love is like a flower bud, so unassuming, so small you'd think it was a dud....then I water it with my love and sprinkle it with Heavens' light, then slowly it grows…....it opens to show all its lovely might your love hides from seeking ears/eyes, so

shy yet so full of sweet loving surprises………you give me gifts everyday, away from prying eyes and 'nah sayers'....your love is like a rare diamond, the more you're pressured to leave, the harder you see to love me...yes, my love, you are a rare find for P - my lover, my S baby, my A diamond, my M*E*..."

~ ~ ~

TASTE OF LOVE
JULY 3, 2012

"I could tasted you a lil' bit, how nice - bitter sweet, like a kiss... must be that love for me inside you I tasted, the things in Me you miss……...everyone is looking to see how long your love for me will endure…....their blocking and waiting, but its that taste of Love that just leaves us wanting more, more , more....I can see u a lil bit, each time your mind meets mine, a vision u just cant 4get - not even in time....must be that soul we share that makes us one, that love connection that's the only thing that can bring us our son....you tasted me a lil' bit last night made me hot, u went on and on and on, as if you never wanted to stop....will there ever be a time when the world will stop looking to see, if we will live my late lovers premonition dream... but what they don't know is we started living the dream when it became you and me...the rest of the dream will come in time, and as in the dream we will live our lives together - like now - Me, yours and you, mine..."

TO MY KNEES
JULY 1, 2012

"Love the way you love me, your sweetness consumes every part of me...... your my protector, my lover, the missing piece of me undercover……...love the way you romance me, your artistry is all the for play I will ever need……..just that 'look' in your eyes would bring me down to my knees ..."

~ ~ ~
CAN'T HELP BUT WIN
JUNE 27, 2012

"Its nobody's business who you love, those that try to control that feeling in others, wish they had IT - the ultimate lover……...Its nobody's business what we say to each other, those that try to listen are haters undercover……..picking and pulling at our words and what they mean, trying to turn them around while trying to destroy our dream......IF they get a chance to find real love they wouldn't want no interfering in what was sent to them from above..... IF they get a chance to feel what we feel, they'll come back one day and apologize for trying to kill...pray for those that try to block what we have between us, lets pray their hearts become full of God's goodness........peeps want others to fail as they did- what a sin, not knowing that when God is behind you, you can not help but win..."

~ ~ ~

BEEN THROUGH IT
JUNE 22, 2012

"We been through several battles so far during our love journey, was wounded but we got back up struggling on our knees..........others tried to stop you - couldn't do that - then they tried to stop me...happened more times than I care to count, but we still got up ready for another round.......your heart is what I love you for, same heart that tries to open, for peeps, opportunity's door...same heart some peeps try to kill at the very core...I wouldn't stop you that's what I love you for, but I have to protect you from their hate, which I cant ignore...we been through battles trying to keep what others dream, constantly awaken by dream-haters not 'feeling' it, it seems... but you never lost sight of me, never looked down on me, now its time to make it so, I'm the only one with you they see...that I'm the only one with you they see" "

~ ~ ~

MUSIC IN ME
JUNE 20, 2012

"Been hearing violins in my ear, cant hear where, really don't care...its making me crazy, taking my emotions here and there……..sweet violins I hear, spinning me round, dipping my body to the ground……..guess its the music in me again, not sure what it all began, the arrival of that so fly sound, but I know it started with the music in you I found..."

~ ~ ~

EMPTY NO LONGER
JUNE 19, 2012

"What a treat you are for me, when I need to feed my eyes, your there....when I need to feed my spirit, you care.... when I need to feed my Soul, you already know.... when I need to feed my hunger, with just your thoughts I'm empty no longer..."

~ ~ ~

DAY DREAM
JUNE 18, 2012

" I day dream of being with you, your backbone, your ear, your hugs when you need someone near…...I day dream of you holding me when I'm in fear, consoling me when I need someone to hear …...just to wake up to your face, hear your voice every day...makes this whole life journey worth while you see...cause I get to love the other part of M*e*."

~ ~ ~

NEVER LOOSING SIGHT
JUNE 17, 2012

"As the sun rises, so does my need for you...just can't do without it, that electric bond between us two...as the sun sets, I remember the last day we met....wouldn't be able to do without you again, love feeling that fire you ignite within....as the moon beams, so does our wildest dreams that have you and I in a passionate lock, blinded by love, but never loosing sight..."

REAL
JUNE 13, 2012

"My heart, I'm feeling you now, its making me swell up in tears, but it confirms we'll never be apart, cause you are here in my heart.........my ribs, knowing the creator made me from you - His ultimate gift that no man can dismiss, my ribs….....my joy, knowing you exist makes my Spirit soar there's nothing like this, my joy……..taking care of you is what I ache to do, hug you when your down, give you so much love, you'd think you've drowned……...my heart, I'm feeling your need for me now, it confirms all that we feel, that your love for me and mine for you is what they call 'real'..."

~ ~ ~

TO THE HEART
JUNE 12, 2012

"Doesn't matter what your height is, what you look like, the tint of your skin - for me I love the man within……..don't matter what your job is, whether your healthy or sick - just so long as you love Music……..real love looks beyond the surface into the heart, for if the heart is good, its guaranteed we'll never  part...doesn't matter if you spend your free time playing video games, as long as you keep burning our love's flame……..for real love looks beyond the lil' issues to the heart - one that's' screaming we'll never be apart'..."

~ ~ ~

YOUR HAPPINESS
JUNE 9, 2012

"When you're happy my heart takes to the seas, I guess that's cause of that link between you and me...when I see your smile, all things seem alright, cause with your smile's light how could we ever fight...your kindness, even in adversity, makes me so proud - its true - cause of that each day I fall deeper in love with you…….when I see evidence of your faithfulness, my love for you grows like a plant reaching towards the light...we're so far in the sky I hold on tight, as we take the lovers' flight……..when your happy my heart sings, my job as your mate is to make sure that never ends, because your happiness, to me and my heart, means everything..."

~ ~ ~

FROM BEHIND
JUNE 7, 2012

"Come sit stay for awhile, as I smother you with kisses and hold you from behind……..that's where I feel comfortable having you as my shield……..like a lion protects his cubs, as they gentle lick their heels……...come sit, stay for awhile as I massage your aching body with my hands... love making you feel good, helping you all I can...that's what I instinctively do, my Love, whenever I'm next to you..."

~ ~ ~

WHAT GOD WANTS
JUNE 5, 2012

"We have to do what we feel God wants us to do, I remember telling that to you……...for no matter what it is we going to, if we have Him in mind, it will pull us through……we have to stand up for the weak and be patience when they fall……..For God in His mercy loves us ALL……but if patience come to an end, so that God's battle we cant win , we need to step aside to let God do this thing…….stepping aside for a minute even a day, gives Him time, a month, maybe weeks to change hearts, and when that day comes we all win, for a Soul was saved and God has made a way out of no way………..we have to do what we feel God wants us to do, for no matter what it is we face in life, He is the only one to pull us through..."

~ ~ ~

SOUL MATE
JUNE 4, 2012

"You can tell a Soul mate anything, cause they are rooted in understanding, understanding of the purpose and heart of conviction, knowing that the choice made is

to only get your attention……….you can let a Soul mate go anywhere alone, cause they are always with you, their moves and feelings are always known………..that's cause a Soul mate already knows what is in their lovers heart, already know no mountain, river or hate storm can ever keep them apart..."

~ ~ ~

LOVE STORY
JUNE 3, 2012

"If it isn't one thing its another, life takes you through pitfalls when we don't learn, 'til you don't want to go any further…...but its love that stops to pick you up, dust you off, teaches you and helps you on your way……..love is there for you before you can fix the words to say …but in a world of many loves, which love do you follow 'til the end, which love do you choose amongst all women……..one with claims to the past or the one with claims to your future…..yes, if it isn't one thing its another, trying to take away the joy we have for each other……..but its love that will win, cause no matter what we are 'love story' until the end..."

~ ~ ~

MAKE WAY FOR THE NEW
JUNE 2, 2012

"Taste my love, take a lil' bit, its sweet and I know you'll love it....feel my love building up inside you too, its looking to find the light shinning in you……..taste my love, take a bite or two...love can change you, take out the hate and rearrange you, and it forgives the past, to make way for a new…"

~ ~ ~

LIGHT HOUSE BEACON
JUNE 1, 2012

"You comfort me with your presence, always there incognito, always the one to care……..I knew it would take someone with your passion for me, to give me what my mind, heart and body been asking…….you comfort me with your smile, always bright, my beacon guiding me home, seen for miles……I knew it would take someone with your heart to stay, stay by my side when all others would have gone away..."

~ ~ ~

THE DREAM
MAY 31, 2012

"So it seems, though its the beginning of you and me, I just realized we living 'the' dream'……..the dream that fore told a man that looks like my past, who holds the key to my future, has finally taken off his mask……..he has 'my 'smile, my humor, my heart, my passions, same style……..the one I was told would give me my hearts maternal desires…….so it seems, though I was whole-now complete, I just realized cause we're too deep in to see, that all along we been living 'the dream'…"

~ ~ ~

THAT DIVE
MAY 30, 2012

" I fell, took that dive risking the blame, but I fell...I choose to dismiss the pain, to hang on to love cause you're doing the  same…..…it was cause of you I fell, cant believe its true, found my dream, my half, my lover in blue ..."

~ ~ ~

MY HOME
MAY 29, 2012

"You are my heart, you came into my world and gave it a new start, now it seems in me my Love- you will always be apart….....you are my smile, you came into my life and stayed for a while, every since you been the center of my world taking me from red to blue, cant even imagine my life lived without you.......you are my future, the moment I looked at you looking at me you became my present, and you're my future unknown, since that day I been longing to make you my home..."

~ ~ ~

ESPECIALLY FOR YOU
MAY 25, 2012

"Its the beat, the way your body feels it, the way your voice sings it - that makes you unique........its the beat, the way it carries your words to the universe, telling of the kind of love we give birth, the kind of love no man can hurt.…....its the beat, the way my body feels it....the way your loving rocks it...that makes me change into something new, something made especially for you..."

~ ~ ~

THE ONE
MAY 24, 2012

"Once in a life time you get to see yourself in the face of someone else...see yourself in their eyes, their words, their talk, their walk and you know, without a doubt, they are the one...the one you can tell your secrets to, the one that makes all endings seem brand new, that one heart that's true...once in a life time you get to see what the other half of you is meant to be...see one that understands your desires and helps you work through your problems...the one you can tell your secrets to, the one that makes all endings brand new, that one - my love - it seems is you...."

~ ~ ~

TAKING ME LOW
MAY 21, 2012

"Taking me low, dipping me slow, you're enslaving my lips like you'll never let go....when I envision your loving , my back is arched as you flow, gently at first, as my orgasm grows….....taking me low, dipping me slow, you're enslaving my heart like you'll never let go...As I feel your loving, your name caresses my lips, as we both hold on to each other slowly rocking our hips....taking you low, dipping you slow, I'm enslaving you lips, and I am never letting 'em go..."

HOW DEEP IS YOUR LOVE
MAY 20, 2012

"How deep is the sea, that's how deep my love is for thee ...a thousand lifetimes could past and begin a new, and my heart would still belong to you…....of your love I will never be full wanting no more, for your love feeds me down to my core..."

~ ~ ~

LIVE IN THE POSITIVE
MAY 19, 2012

"I don't live in the negative, I live in the positive……..get hot for me not from my reaction to the hate your Xs bring, but from the love I give cause it means everything……..you may not know of that kind of love so hot it ignites, cause you're so use to the hate, distrust fussing your Xs brought to your life……....once you shed that past, close that door you'll bond with me so tight, you will know of the world of God's light, one that will take you to unbelievable new heights..."…

~ ~ ~

MY ANGEL
MAY 15, 2012

"One day I saw in my home a black and gold butterfly as bright as the sun and I wondered with excite-

ment from where did it come……..I wanted to know the meaning of this...I learned Biblically it means a change, and worldly it meant a visit...so beautiful it was, but without knowing I opened the door and let it go....now I believe that butterfly was you, so gentle a heart, easily manipulated by the dark…...yet, as with the butterfly you are changing, just like me...one of Gods precious creatures too kind to see, how heartless the world can be, so I protect you - my angel watching over me..."

~ ~ ~

MIRROR IMAGE
MAY 14, 2012

"Sleep was my old friend, use to visit me 'til dawn... but when my late suddenly passed, next thing I know my old friend Sleep was gone...Guess I couldn't see Sleep when another disaster I might find...had to make sure I was awake and prepared for the next time....but then you came into my life, a mirror image of my stolen past, a past that I thought i could never have...you possessed first my Soul, you willed me to 'see' you, so you could tell me 'this is mine'...then you loved me mentally and emotionally treating me like a rare find, so sweet you are, it seems my old friend Sleep has given me some time..."...

~ ~ ~

LISTEN TO LOVE
MAY 12, 2012

"Stop, listen...its the sound of my heart beating fast...happens every time I realized your my future and now my  past……..stop, listen...its the sound of our laughter...happens every time we talk, our love grows faster and faster……...stop, listen...its our love building up speed...moving down hill, each day until the only thing anyone can do, is just get out of our way..."

~ ~ ~

ANGEL OF MINE
MAY 10, 2012

"Its exciting and scary all at the same time...this love, this miracle, you, that angel of mine...its destiny and yet unbelievable, what we possess is like a raw gem sought by all men...all the dots that connect us, all our experiences brought us here you see...to a place where we follow and God's Love leads..."

~ ~ ~

BRAND NEW
MAY 9, 2012

"Every thought I have involves you, the one I'd spend my life being true to……..because of your love for me and your smile, I now pray when next you come, that you'll stay for a while……..everything I see, I see with new eyes, everything's brand new, every second I live is now spent missing you..."

~ ~ ~

HOME IN YOUR ARMS
MAY 7, 2012

"Home is where the heart is my home is by your side, a place where both our thoughts and feelings coincide…….cuff you up, throw away the key, as you said, your house is not a home unless you are there with me...I been up since 3, sleep also alluded me, caused me alarm...until I realized you woke me up cause you want me in your arms..."

ONE
MAY 4, 2012

"My Love you're always on my mind...when I see you, I see me...when I sing, I see us in every song...am I wrong guess that's love... the kind that makes you smile at every one, the kind that makes you believe two can become one..."

~ ~ ~

CLINGING TO ME
APRIL 29, 2012

"I know you feel me I know you care, I know sometimes life is just not going to be fair.......you know I adore you, you know my needs, you know there are those that don't want us to succeed......but love is the bond that connects us, a bond that many cant see, they cant understand why your still clinging to me..."

~ ~ ~

UNSTOPPABLE US
APRIL 28, 2012

"I love how you care for me, my every thought and even my feelings, you can see....i love that you are proud of me, my past, my present, what I've chosen to be...just keep your focus on building up my trust and together we will be, the unstoppable US..."

~ ~ ~

WINDOWS TO MY SOUL
APRIL 26, 2012

"My eyes are the window to my Soul, in yours I see my future, a future that only you know........in your eyes I see my heart, in there lays my life, my light in the dark.......together we're the strength of a 100 men - forever we will sing, so pure so bold - together we can do just about anything..."

~ ~ ~

EVERY MAN HAS A WOMAN
APRIL 24, 2012

"I ache for your presence, your touch, your lips to taste, I long for the day when the world can see what God has made.........what will they say when they find out we're Soul mates, that we're living proof no matter the age - for every man a woman God has made..."

~ ~ ~

MY WORLD IS UNKNOWN
APRIL 20, 2012

"You travel in a group, I travel alone........you have the world at your feet my world is unknown, yet our worlds meet and they fit perfectly, cause I bring the solitude and you bring me heat..."

~ ~ ~

THE LUCKY ONE
APRIL 19, 2012

"Takes one look, one heart, one light to make you stop in your tracks and change your life.........takes real love, real trust, real love-making, makes you go beyond comfort - never forsaking..........you found me when I thought I was done, you showed me the magnitude of this love - you showed me I'm the lucky one..."

~ ~ ~

WHEN I SING
APRIL 17, 2012

"My heart is full cause you give me 100...it makes me want to sing 'he's the perfect lover'...you show the world I got your full attention, have me singing 'he's the perfect father for a

son'...your voice, your eyes, your vibes give back to me one thing, the ability to use my gift from God, the ability to move people when I sing..."

~ ~ ~

THIS SMILE PEOPLE SEE
APRIL 15, 2012

"You cause this smile people see on my face, your loving, your patience, your devotion, you just cant be replaced...you cause this heart of mine to open up to care again, your hope, your voice, your style...that's why we will always win...no mountain, no person, no wall, no matter what they do, nothing will make me ever stop loving you..."

~ ~ ~

TRIED TO KILL
APRIL 14, 2012

"My smile means you've touch my heart, you've fed my trust to ensure an 'US'....my smile is me, its how I feel, you've given it back, what your Xs tried to kill...your smile means I've touch your heart, I've fed your trust to ensure 'loving me is a must'.....your smile is you, its how you feel, our love has given it back, what your Xs tried to kill…"

~ ~ ~

INSIDE OF ME
APRIL 12, 2012

"I feel your love, your thoughts I see
...for your body lives inside of me"

~ ~ ~

A LOVE THAT HANGS
APRIL 10, 2012

"Sometimes its hard to believe in love when the world is so heartless, cant seem to find anyone that's not part of all this.........you try and you try, but it seems everyone falls short, until that day you meet who God sent you here for.........that person feels your passion and respects your space.........someone that talks instead of shout, someone that holds you instead of fight........a love that hangs on to you - wont move their feet, even if it means no more heartbeat..."

~ ~ ~

THEY CAN'T FEEL IT
APRIL 8, 2012

"One thing I can't deny is all the love I see in your eyes...just can't say in words how your love keeps me satisfied….....people try to steal it, block it, kill it...but they don't know cause they can't feel it….....don't feel that our love can't be denied, its a burning flame until the day we die..."

~ ~ ~

YOUR MUSIC
APRIL 2, 2012

"I am your Music, let your music take you, fill you up and make you, let you music guide you when you can't see behind you....... let your Music built you up when you're weak, lift you and show you what you cant see - just focus on me........I am your Music, I'm all you need and that's a fact, because your Music will always have your back..."

~ ~ ~

NO WORDS TO EXPRESS
MARCH 21, 2012

"When there are no words to express what you want to say, the look in your eyes tell me lead the way……..when your mind is clouded by things people do and say,. your heart cries out to me I cant see please lead the way please………what a sweet heart you have, so gentle and needy, in every way, no wonder you cant do without me, not even for a day.."

~ ~ ~

LIKE BRUCE LEE
MARCH 12, 2012

"People think men are blind to the emotions we women feel, that they cant see, but I say its a man with a kind heart that feels 'just as deep' ...and he is the essence of Godly men, for he will love a faithful woman until the very end….…..people say men can be persuaded by the beauty they see, but I say its the man with a heart of gold that knows the vision of beauty goes past the skin, that its 'just that deep'...when our hearts are united for good, what a powered union that will be, cause the strength of our two Souls - that will match perfectly - will become unbeatable as the legendary Bruce Lee..."

~ ~ ~

BEYOND DOPE
MARCH 6, 2012

"Always remember in times when it gets too hard, what we each found and how special God must think we are...He give us something people may not experience in a life time, to feel another's' heart beat only few will find...I hope that precious gift we were given gives you strength and hope, that the love we share is indescribable - beyond dope and my Love as long as you breath I'll be here so 'always' have hope..."

~ ~ ~

MY MAN
MARCH 4, 2012

"Take a little time and breath, stop the world and just think of me........take a little time to see, that the 'I' and the 'me' has turned into 'we'........feel it coming, its coming soon, like a melody comes with a special tune........the day will come when you can tell anyone you can, that I'm your lady and you are my man..."

~ ~ ~

YOU AND ME
MARCH 1, 2012

"When you love someone you want them happy even if that happiness is without you……...When you love someone you want to protect their heart from people and words that will give them pain………..even if protecting them means a life without you...Sometimes the heart gets blinded by what it wants, not what it needs, when it should be focusing on what those it loves want - and not so much on the what about 'me'...God calls it the sin nature, the me, me, me...what about me train-of-thought ...it blinds you to His gift that you now cant see cause you  focused on 'me'....When God gives you a gift that you reject and mistreat...He takes it back and gives it to someone who knows what a blessing you can be...Gives the first a testimony so they will never repeat and it gives the second a reward for paying the cost for being true to Love even when all hope was lost....so when life gets hard and you see no way through, just think of the magical gift God has given to you...cause He knew of all people - us two - could be that beacon of light that will cause the world to see....that the purest of love is REAL and it can be seen in you and me..." -

~ ~ ~

TAKES ONE TO KNOW ONE
FEBRUARY 27, 2012

"Takes wisdom to know wisdom, takes a pure heart to see one........took your love's light to guide me to this place, where I can love free from criticism and still feel safe........takes faith in love to continue to keep what others want to kill, takes our love for one another to anticipate how each other feels.........takes passion to create passion inside of me, takes faith in what I see to learn this love will always be..."

~ ~ ~

LIKE TEA
FEBRUARY 24, 2012

"I need you like the fish need the waters, like an army needs its orders, I need you...I feel you like a masseuse feels his clients, like you feel who I am, I feel you...I love you like God loves us unconditionally, like the English love their morning tea …"

~ ~ ~

TIME IS NOW
FEBRUARY 16, 2012

"Sometimes ain't no turning back cause the future is where we're at…... ain't no turning back cause the past is gone and that's a fact, our time is now so lets experience the full-love impact..."

~ ~ ~

PURE LOVE
JANUARY 30, 2012

"You know its pure love when a man is willing to give up an empire, you know its pure love when a woman will forsake all others to lift a man higher.......cause pure love is unlike the imitating frauds, it comes with an unconditional warranty cause its backed by God"

~ ~ ~

I CAN FEEL
JANUARY 12, 2013

"I can feel when you're busy I sit back and I don't fear, cause I know as sure as the sunrises I will feel you coming near......I'm the same way when I am busy as things occupy my mind, in the midst I stop and reach for you across space and time...........I rest my head on your chest I'm sure you can feel me there, cause I feel you do the same to mine our hearts beating at the same time.......you know we have similar chests, yours of a man and mine a woman's breast.......yours is hard and brings me protection, and mine bring you a soft place for resting........I can feel when you're busy but I sit back and I don't fear, for I know your love will be with me forever and always close and near..."

~ ~ ~

LIKE A GLOVE
JANUARY 13, 2013

"All we have is now, tomorrow is gone and the future is yet to be carve and won.......we'll living in the now matured, strengthen and multiplied by love, fitting perfectly together has a hand does in a glove........not even time, people, distance, and circumstance have lessened the bond we created, like LL Cool J

we just 'so elated'.......yes all we have is now tomorrow is gone and the future is yet to be lived, so for now to you my Love all my heart I give..."

~ ~ ~

EVERYONE KNOWS
JANUARY 12, 2013

"Everyone knows you love Me, that's what you said one day and I believe........even Stevie Wonder can see the love that flows from you to me, that's why I believe......people who notice question cause they just cant believe, that someone like you could love a women like me......but who in their right mind would stop that love flow, so beautiful it looks on us,  that the world has stop to look, Love has become contagious........so why put up road blocks, cause love will just take another direction you see, they do it just so it looks like they are Me when everybody knows and believe...."

~ ~ ~

PROTECT EACH OTHER FROM EVIL
JANUARY 11, 2013

"It takes a village they say to raise a child, I believe that attitude will take us further than a mile........but people are afraid of this crazy world so in a group they tend to live in, we follow the leader and close our doors and ears to sin

…….. but that child or person we turn over to evil- turn a blind eye to - will grow up one day and do the same to you.........we all are one big family - children of the most High Lord, and what we don't see is when we protect each other from evil - we're standing up for God ……..it takes a village they say to raise a child so take the time to feed, take a risk and protect them no matter what it is that they need........ a minute to give them love that their missing or to discipline even if you have to suffer a while, cause for them that means there's hope in this world - even if what you give is just a smile..."

~ ~ ~

YOUR LADY
JANUARY 6, 2013

"Your lady, that's what they'll call me your one and only lady, the one that's good at nurturing you and your babies.........the one that pleases your mind, body and Soul, the one lady you long to for- ever hold........my man, that's what they'll call you and I'll do the same, the one that loves me so much he don't mind me carrying his name.........the only one that pleases my mind, body and Soul, the one man I will forever long to hold..."

~ ~ ~

VIOLINS
JANUARY 10, 2013

"I'm hearing violins crying in and out passions running high, until the sound of the violin strings reaches high above the sky.......its followed by a big drum roll, warning of treasures untold......a melody so sweet so kind, born of a genius, you, the supreme mastermind......hearing violins again picking up its step as its' strings are plucked, its causing me to dance and dance 'til I just can't get enough..."

~ ~ ~

OONE MANNLY MAN I SEE
JANUARY 9, 2013

"Hold me take control, be the only man I see, what a relief to know someone is being the man God wants him to be....... provider, protector, best friend, lover and admirer, someone that makes you want to reach higher and higher.......I'll have your back and you'll have mine, nothing but love as God has de-signed......always warning each other when bad-news is coming, and when it arrives we give noth-

ing but loving......hold me take control, be my ying to my yang, be my light in my dark, my driver in my one-man lane..."

~ ~ ~

AN ICON
JANUARY 24, 2013

"You are an icon, forever there will be the mention of the one, the one who took a song about underwear and made it fun......so no matter what your battles just know you've already won, for it seems we will be forever be singing your lyrics and dancing to your song ....and when ever there is talk about releasing the passion within, we will always refer to it as the release of the Dragon'....for everything artistic you do is destined for greatness, cause not many like you are able to take it........you are an icon you belong to the world, and I respect that as your one and only girl..."

~ ~ ~

ROAD THE WAVE ON A BOARD
JANUARY 23, 2013

"I saw 2 lives being lived through you, one thrust upon and the other a dream come true…..until that dream came the other life just took control, as you searched and search for that 'special' someone to hold.......then through a crowded sea you saw the one with the chemistry, and suddenly  you knew that 'special' someone was me.........you reached out and asked could we date, I said yes but I must be the only one in your lake.......like the best strategy you took over the DJ booth, and bravely hit everyone with the rareness of truth.......yes there was backlash that came in the form of a "sucka" punch, but you did your Michael Jackson moves as we lovingly became one.......you changed the mood with the music and the beat as we rode the wave on a board called the truth, we couldn't have made it if it wasn't for you - that day you took control of the DJ Booth..."

~ ~ ~

SILVER CROSS
MARCH 25, 2013

"Never really looked at the fact that we both wear 'chains' until God opened my eyes, I've been wearing long and short cross chains seems like all my life..........to me the cross is a symbol of His sacrifice, that no matter how many times we slip into darkness He is always there to show us the light...........my favorite chain is silver, silver ear rings and silver chains, reminds me of  platinum being ahead of the game.............tears came to my eyes when I saw you wearing your cross chain again, I know its just a symbol as is the ring, but that cross on you it just means everything..."

...The Journey Continues...

(Photos and graphics not the authors is courtesy of www.Pixabay.com)

Author
Eunice Moseley

Eunice Moseley has over 28 years experience as a journalist. She started at *The Baltimore Times* in 1986as a writer/reporter for Community features, and later was promoted to entertainment editor. She currently serves there as Promotions Director (at-large). Moseley is owner and president of at Freelance Associates, a public relations/business management consulting Company. It was established in 1993.

In 1990 she launched a syndicated column, *The Pulse of Entertainment* (www.ThePulseofEntertainment.com). It currently has a combined estimated readership each week of 1/4 million. This includes syndicated placement on such media outlets as *Houston Style Magazine, The Buffalo Criterion,* www.EURweb.com, www.KJLHRadio.com, and www.AtlantaDailyWorld.com .

Even though Moseley suffers from dyslexia she holds a Bachelors in Telecommunications from Morgan State University, two Masters from University of Maryland's University College in Management Technology/Public Relations and an M.B.A., and she is currently in a PhD program at Walden University in Management - Leadership and Organizational Change.

The Baltimore native recently accepted a contractual teaching position at California State University (Los Angeles) in Management. She is also founder (1999) and coordination of a annual free entertainment conference, "Uplifting Minds II," held in Baltimore and Hollywood (www.UpliftingMinds2.com).

Freelance Associates Publications
Long Beach, CA. FreeAssocInc3@aol.com. 562-424-3836.
www.ThePulseofEntertainment.com

www.ingramcontent.com/pod-product-compliance
Lightning Source LLC
Chambersburg PA
CBHW042055290426
44111CB00001B/13